FIRST EDITION

Edited By: **Kelly Hanton**

Designed By: **Anthony Brown** and **Natalie Lindsey**

All rights reserved.

No part of this book may be reproduced or transmitted in any form or by any means, electronic or mechanical, including photocopying, recording, or by any information storage and retrieval system, without written permission from the publisher.

Under no circumstance will any blame or legal responsibility be held against the author for any damages, reparation or loss due to the information contained within this book, including but not limited to, errors, omissions or inaccuracies either directly or indirectly.

Acknowledgments

Writing this book has been a journey, and I wouldn't have reached the finish line without the support of many incredible people.

First and foremost, my deepest gratitude goes to my **[partner Sophia Ava]**, who provided unwavering encouragement, endless cups of coffee, and sanity checks throughout the writing process. Their love and patience were invaluable.

My sincere thanks to my **editor, [Kelly Hanton]**, for your keen eye, insightful suggestions, and guidance in shaping this book. Your expertise made a world of difference.

I am also grateful to my agents, for believing in this project and helping me navigate the publishing world. Your support and professionalism were instrumental.

Many thanks to my **friends and colleagues** who offered feedback on early drafts, shared their knowledge, and celebrated the milestones with me. Your enthusiasm and support kept me motivated.

A special thank you to **[anyone who provided specific help, e.g., research assistance, illustrations, blurbs]**. Your contribution is greatly appreciated.

Finally, thank you to the **readers**. This book exists for you. I hope you find it informative, inspiring, or simply enjoyable.

CONTENT

1   How to use this Book

4   Introduction

5   Geology, History and Wildlife

7   How to Prepare

10   Map

Hiking

Easy Hikes

12   Boardwalk Trail

30   Bluff Trail

41   Sims Trail

50   Bates Ferry Trail

Moderate Hikes

60   Weston Lake Trail

72   Fork Swamp Trail

Difficult Hikes

81   Oakridge Trail

93   River Trail

104   Kingsnake Trail

116   Glossary

How to use this Book

The first section of the book is a layout map. This map depicts the natural features of the land, including mountains, valleys, trails, and bodies of water. By studying the map, you can plan your route, estimate the distance and elevation gain, and anticipate any challenging terrain.

By using a compass together with this guide, you can determine locations and navigate through unfamiliar terrain. This is especially important if you veer off course or encounter unexpected obstacles.

The section on hiking covers crucial aspects of a hiking trail

Including:

- **Trailhead location**
- **Description**
- **Difficulty**
- **Day Hike/Multi Day Hike**
- **Dog/Kid Friendly**
- **Type of hike**
- **Elevation change**
- **Length**
- **Estimated time to complete**
- **Features**
- **Allowed uses**
- **Best time to hike**
- **Tips**

It is important to note that some of these parameters may vary depending on several aspects:

Trail Length

A trail length depends on the starting point and end point used when measuring and may vary from one source to another. At times trail lengths can change over time due to erosion, rerouting, or construction.

The way the trail length is measured can vary. Some sources might use a GPS track, which could account for every twist and turn, while others might rely on a ranger's estimate or a historical map, which might be less precise.

Difficulty

The difficulty of a trail is typically determined by a combination of factors, including:

Terrain: How rough or smooth is the path? Is it mostly dirt, rock, roots, or pavement? Are there obstacles like streams, boulders, or steep drop-offs?

Elevation gain: How much climbing is involved? A steeper or longer climb will be more difficult.

Distance: How far is the total hike? A longer hike will naturally require more endurance.

Exposure: Are there sections of the trail where you'll be high up and at risk of a fall, with no railing or protection?

Trailhead location

Trailhead location might be moved due to many reasons some common factors are:

Safety: This is a big one. If the area around the old trailhead becomes unsafe due to things like erosion, flooding, or danger from falling rocks, park services might have to reroute the trail to a new starting point.

Conservation: Sometimes, a trailhead needs to be moved to protect the environment. If the old trailhead was disturbing wildlife habitat or a sensitive ecosystem, park rangers might create a new trailhead in a less disruptive location.

Estimated time to complete

There are many reasons why estimates for hiking trail completion times can vary so much, even for the same trail. Most common reasons are:

Hiker ability: This is a big one. An experienced hiker with good fitness will move much faster than someone new to hiking or who is out of shape.

Trail conditions: Mud, snow, rocks, and overgrown trails can all slow you down considerably. Weather can also play a big role - rain, wind, and extreme heat can all make a hike more difficult.

Pace: Are you stopping often to take breaks or pictures? Are you hiking with a group that needs to go slower than you might like? All of this can affect your overall time.

Elevation gain: This is a big one - the more elevation you gain, the longer it will take to complete the hike.

Taking breaks: Factoring in breaks for lunch, taking photos, or just enjoying the view is important. Don't forget to schedule some rest time into your hike.

There is a section for Trail Maps divided into sites and descriptions of what is available at each site.

Every effort has been made by the author and editors to make this guide as accurate as possible. However, many things can change after a guide is published i.e. trails may be rerouted or washed away by nature, roads may be closed and many other possibilities. **WE HOPE ALL THE USERS UNDERSTAND THIS!!**

Introduction

Imagine a world where towering trees pierce the sky like ancient sentinels, their branches intertwined to form a verdant canopy that blocks out the sun. Where the air is thick with the sweet scent of decaying leaves and the symphony of countless creatures fills your ears. This is Congaree National Park, a hidden gem nestled in the heart of South Carolina.

As you venture into this lush wilderness, you'll find yourself dwarfed by the towering bald cypress trees, their trunks gnarled and twisted with age. These majestic giants, some over 1,200 years old, are the heart and soul of the park. Their roots, exposed and intertwined, create a labyrinthine network known as a "kneeland," a testament to the park's unique ecosystem.

The park's floodplain forests, known as pocosins, are another marvel to behold. These unique wetlands are characterized by their dense understory of shrubs and vines, which create a nearly impenetrable tangle. As you navigate through this labyrinth, you'll encounter a variety of fascinating plants, including carnivorous sundew and pitcher plants, which have adapted to the nutrient-poor soil by trapping and digesting insects.

Congaree National Park is also a haven for wildlife. Keep your eyes peeled for deer, raccoons, and opossums as you hike through the forest. If you're lucky, you may even catch a glimpse of a red-shouldered hawk soaring overhead or a cottonmouth snake slithering through the undergrowth. The park's waterways are home to a variety of fish, including largemouth bass, catfish, and bream, making it a popular destination for anglers.

But it's not just the wildlife that makes Congaree National Park so special. The park's serene atmosphere and stunning beauty have a way of calming the soul. As you hike through the forest, take a moment to appreciate the simple things in life: the rustle of leaves in the wind, the song of a bird, the warmth of the sun on your skin.

Whether you're a seasoned hiker or simply looking for a peaceful escape from the hustle and bustle of everyday life, Congaree National Park is a must-visit destination. So lace up your boots, grab your backpack, and prepare to be amazed by the natural wonders of this incredible place.

Geology, History & Wildlife

Congaree National Park stands as a testament to the intricate interplay of geological forces, human history, and natural biodiversity. Its unique landscape, shaped by the confluence of the Congaree and Wateree rivers, is a living museum of ancient processes and a thriving ecosystem.

A Geological Tapestry

The park's foundation is rooted in the dynamic history of the Coastal Plain. Over millennia, the relentless ebb and flow of rivers, coupled with sea-level changes, have sculpted the floodplain into its current form. The deposition of sediments, rich in nutrients, has created a fertile environment that supports a diverse array of plant life. The park's towering trees, including the majestic bald cypress and live oak, are a testament to this nutrient-rich soil.

Geological features such as oxbow lakes, meanders, and floodplains are evidence of the river's powerful influence. These features have created a mosaic of habitats, from dense forests to open wetlands, providing a sanctuary for a variety of species. The park's geological diversity is further enhanced by the presence of ancient floodplain terraces, which offer a glimpse into the region's past.

A Historical Crossroads

Congaree National Park has been a crossroads of human history for centuries. Native American tribes, including the Catawba and Yemassee, inhabited the region, relying on its natural resources for sustenance. European settlers arrived in the 17th century, drawn by the fertile land and navigable waterways. The park's floodplain forests were cleared for agriculture and timber, leaving a lasting impact on the landscape.

Despite the challenges of human settlement, portions of the floodplain remained intact. These remnants of old-growth forest, now protected within the park, offer a glimpse into the region's pre-colonial state. The park's historical significance is also reflected in its archaeological sites, which provide evidence of human activity dating back thousands of years.

A Wildlife Haven

Congaree National Park is a haven for a diverse range of wildlife. The park's floodplain forests and wetlands provide essential habitat for numerous species, including mammals, birds, reptiles, amphibians, and fish. Visitors may encounter deer, wild boar, and raccoons as they explore the park's trails. The park is also a birdwatcher's paradise, with over 200 species having been recorded.

The park's unique ecosystem supports a variety of endangered and threatened species, such as the wood stork and the red-cockaded woodpecker. Conservation efforts are focused on protecting these species and restoring their habitat. Congaree National Park's commitment to wildlife conservation has made it a vital refuge for biodiversity in the southeastern United States.

How to Prepare

Before You Go:

- **Research:** Familiarize yourself with the park's attractions, trails, and activities. Explore the official website for detailed information on park hours, fees, and current conditions.

- **Book Accommodations:** Choose from nearby hotels, cabins, or campgrounds. If camping, make reservations well in advance, especially during peak seasons.

- **Obtain Permits:** For backcountry camping or specific activities like firefly viewing, obtain the necessary permits.

- **Check Weather and Conditions:** Monitor the weather forecast and park updates for any closures or advisories due to flooding or other factors.

When to Visit:

- **Spring (March-May):** Enjoy pleasant weather, blooming wildflowers, and the opportunity to witness the annual firefly phenomenon.

- **Summer (June-August):** Experience lush greenery and abundant wildlife but be prepared for higher temperatures and humidity.

- **Fall (September-November):** Enjoy cooler temperatures, vibrant fall foliage, and fewer crowds.

- **Winter (December-February):** Experience a quieter park with opportunities for birdwatching and hiking.

Getting There:

- **By Car:** Congaree National Park is located approximately 20 miles from Columbia, South Carolina. Follow Interstate 77 or Interstate 26 to reach the park.
- **By Air:** The nearest major airport is Columbia Metropolitan Airport (CAE). From there, you can rent a car or take a taxi to the park.

What to Pack:

- **Comfortable Clothing:** Pack lightweight, breathable clothing suitable for hiking, camping, and varying weather conditions.
- **Footwear:** Sturdy hiking boots or trail runners are essential for exploring the park's trails.
- **Insect Repellent:** Protect yourself from mosquitoes, ticks, and other insects, especially during the warmer months.
- **Sunscreen:** Shield yourself from the sun, especially during the summer.
- **Water and Snacks:** Stay hydrated and fueled during your adventures.
- **First Aid Kit:** Be prepared for minor injuries or ailments.
- **Camera:** Capture the park's stunning scenery and wildlife.
- **Binoculars:** Enhance your wildlife viewing experience.

Things to Do:

- **Hiking:** Explore the park's network of trails, ranging from easy to challenging. Don't miss the Boardwalk Loop Trail, which offers scenic views of the floodplain forest.

- **Camping:** Experience the tranquility of nature by camping in one of the park's campgrounds.

- **Canoeing and Kayaking:** Paddle through the park's waterways and enjoy the peaceful atmosphere.

- **Fishing:** Try your luck at fishing in the park's creeks and rivers.

- **Wildlife Viewing:** Keep an eye out for a variety of wildlife, including deer, alligators, turtles, and various bird species.

- **Ranger-Led Programs:** Participate in guided hikes, talks, and other programs to learn more about the park's natural and cultural history.

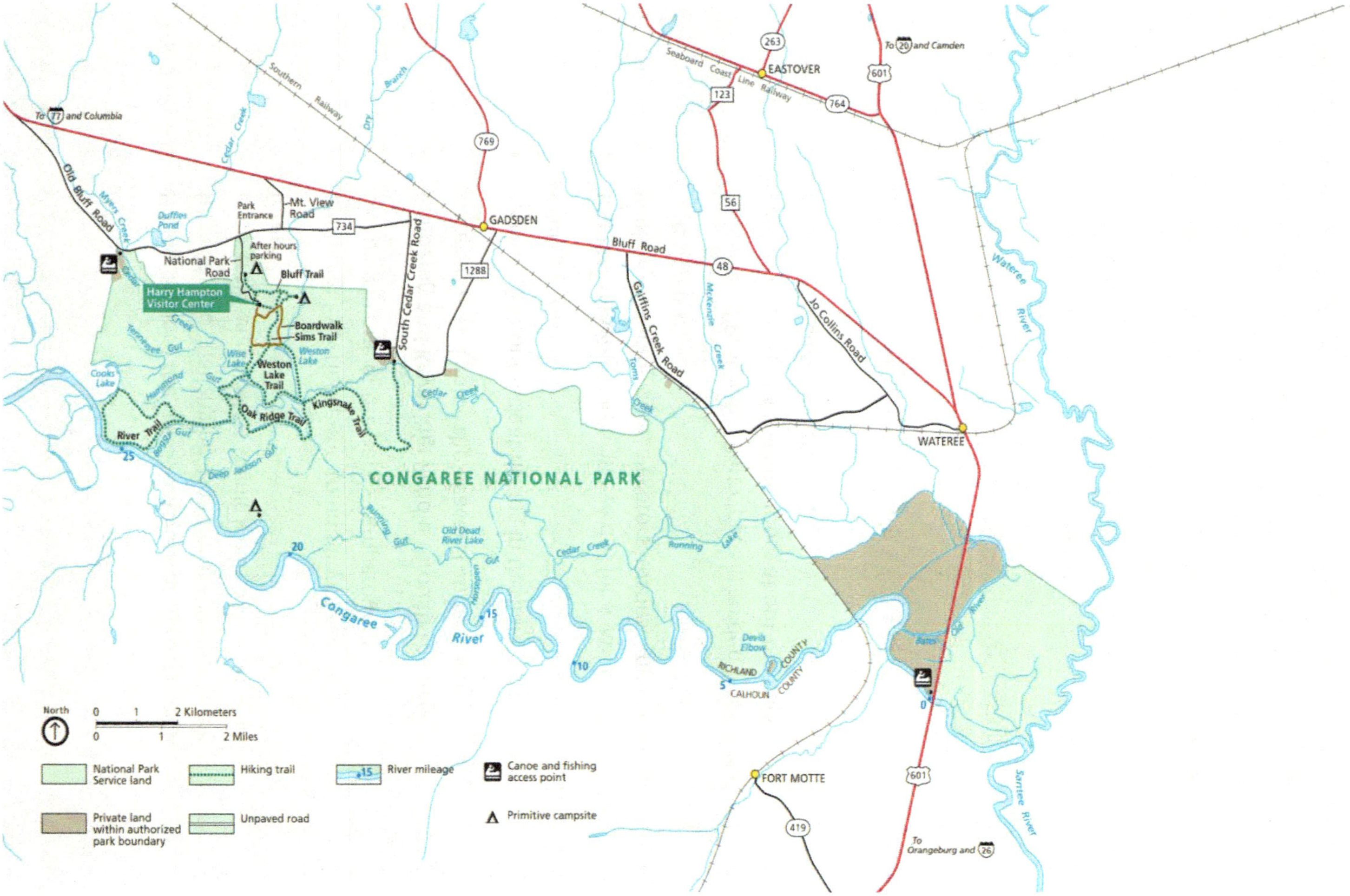
CONGAREE NATIONAL PARK
To 77 and Columbia
Old Bluff Road
Myers Creek
Duffies Pond
Cedar Creek
Southern Railway
Dry Branch
Park Entrance
Mt. View Road
734
769
GADSDEN
National Park Road
After hours parking
Bluff Trail
Harry Hampton Visitor Center
Boardwalk
Sims Trail
Weston Lake
Wise Lake
Weston Lake Trail
Tennessee Gut
Cooks Lake
Hammond Gut
Oak Ridge Trail
Kingsnake Trail
River Trail
Boggy Gut
Deep Jackson Gut
South Cedar Creek Road
1288
Bluff Road
48
Griffins Creek Road
Toms Creek
McKenzie Creek
Jo Collins Road
56
123
263
EASTOVER
Seaboard Coast Line Railway
764
601
To 20 and Camden
Wateree River
WATEREE
Running Gut
Old Dead River Lake
Horsepen Gut
Running Lake
Congaree River
25
20
15
10
5
0
Devils Elbow
RICHLAND COUNTY
CALHOUN COUNTY
Bates Old River
FORT MOTTE
419
Santee River
To Orangeburg and 26
North
0 1 2 Kilometers
0 1 2 Miles
National Park Service land
Private land within authorized park boundary
Hiking trail
Unpaved road
River mileage
Canoe and fishing access point
Primitive campsite

Congaree National Park Trail Map

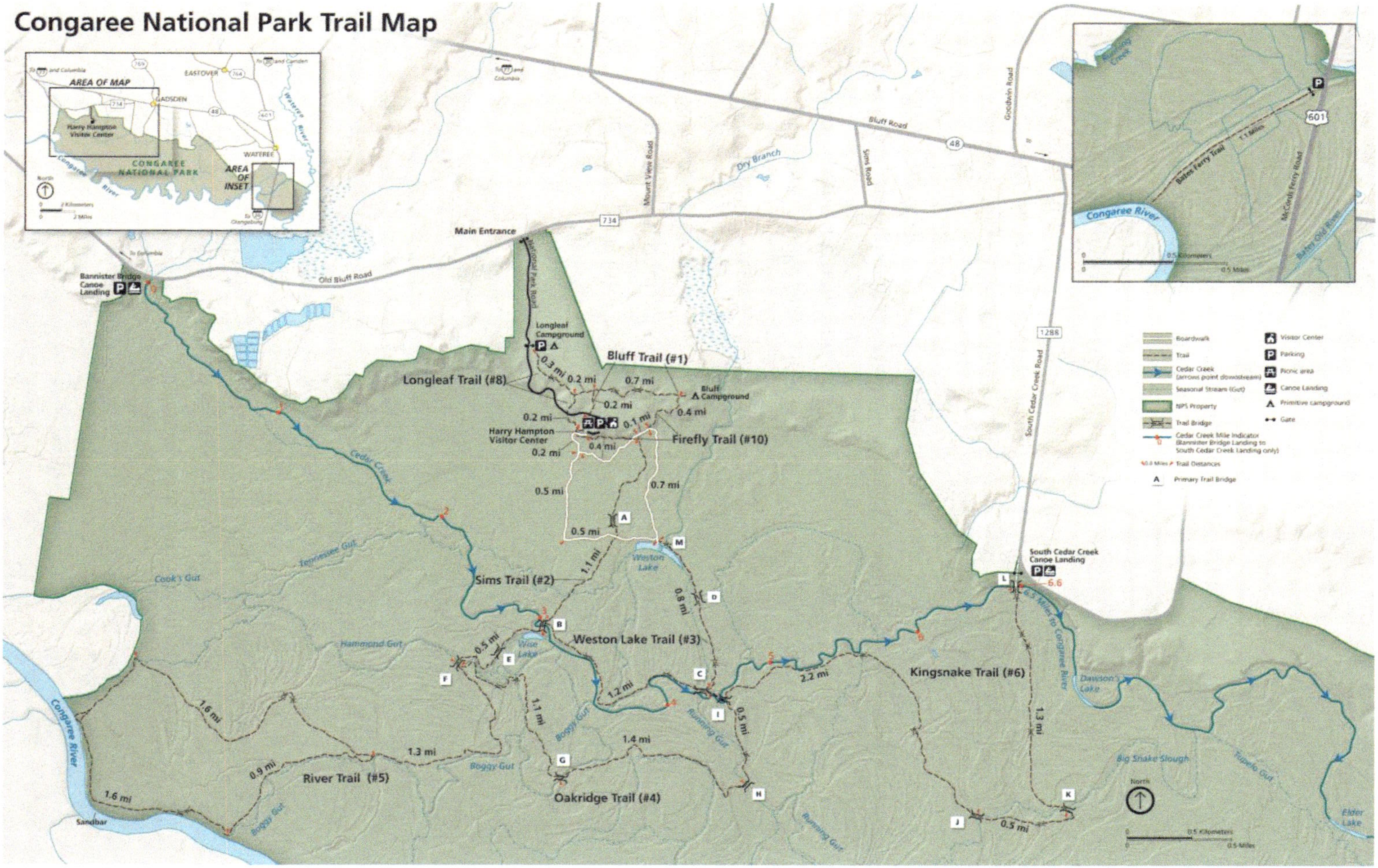

Hiking

Hiking trails are assigned numbers, which appear on reflective blazes attached to trees and posts. To assist with navigation, approximately every one-tenth of a mile, there will be a blaze with GPS coordinates. Be aware that storms can bring down trees and the trail markers with them. Always pay close attention to your surroundings as you navigate in the forest.

Easy Hikes

Boardwalk Trail

Trailhead:

The trailhead is located at the Harry Hampton Visitor Center in Congaree National Park which is open daily from 9:00 AM to 5:00 PM.

Description:

This 2.4-mile hike takes visitors through a variety of habitats, showcasing the park's natural and cultural history.

One of the highlights of the trail is the opportunity to see towering trees, including loblolly pine, beech, and baldcypress. These giants are a testament to the park's unique environment and have played a significant role in its designation as a national park. As you walk along the boardwalk, you'll also pass through a cypress-tupelo flat, where cypress "knees" emerge from the floodplain soils. At the Weston Lake overlook, keep an eye out for turtles, sunfish, and gar.

The trail also offers a glimpse into the park's history of natural disturbances. Evidence of hurricanes, ice storms, and floods can be seen throughout the old-growth forest. In the later part of the hike, you'll pass through ideal habitat for the rare Carolina bogmint, which blooms in mid-summer.

While Congaree National Park may be a relatively new national park, it has a rich cultural history. The land has been inhabited by many peoples over the centuries, and while their presence may be subtle, it is still evident in the landscape.

In addition to the natural and cultural features, the boardwalk trail also offers excellent opportunities for wildlife viewing. Red-shouldered hawks and barred owls often nest near the trail, and visitors may be lucky enough to see these predators hunting for crayfish and other prey. The park is also home to a variety of other bird species, including pileated woodpeckers, red-headed woodpeckers, and chimney swifts. Keep an eye out for box turtles, mud turtles, and rat snakes near the bluff. And don't forget to look for skinks, anoles, and caterpillars, which can be fascinating for both children and adults.

Boardwalk Trail Map

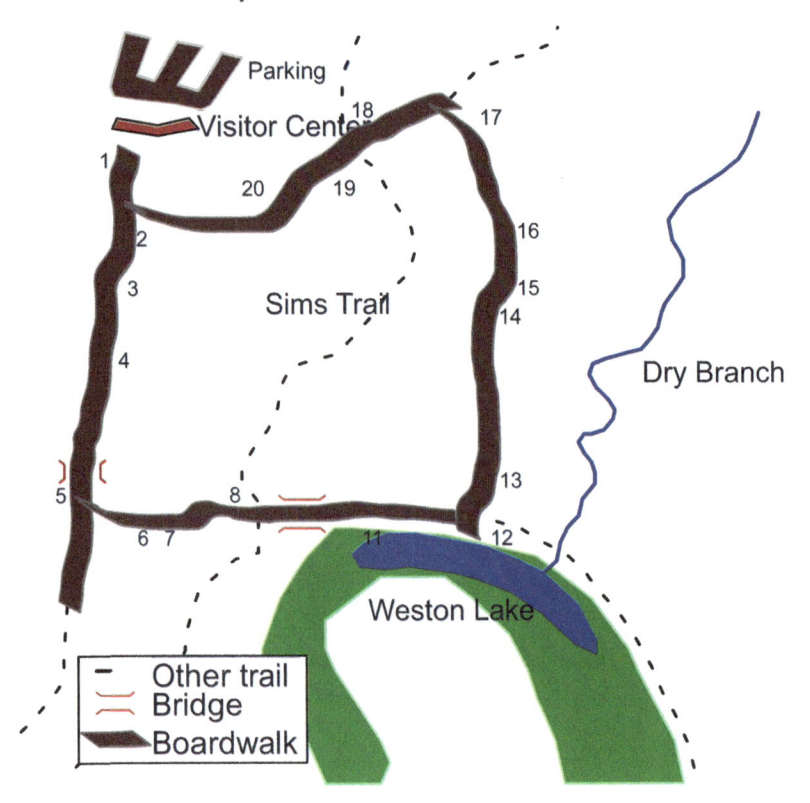

Site 1: American Beech Tree

This majestic tree, with its smooth, light gray bark, is a native species to South Carolina. It can reach impressive heights of up to 115 feet and forms a dense canopy, providing shade and shelter for the forest's inhabitants. American beeches thrive in moist, loamy soils, making them a reliable indicator of fertile land. Historically, settlers used these trees as a sign of good soil for cultivation.

Within the park, the American beech trees are commonly found on the bluff and higher ridges of floodplains. They are unable to tolerate prolonged periods of wet, anaerobic conditions. These trees produce small, brown nuts enclosed in spiky, angular husks. These edible nuts are a valuable food source for birds and squirrels, and have been historically used as a food source by Native Americans.

Site 2: Muck Swamp

As you continue your journey toward Site 2, pay close attention to the changes in the soil and vegetation. The boardwalk traverses a unique ecosystem known as a muck swamp. This type of wetland is characterized by its thick, dense layer of soil composed of clay and peat. This muck acts as a natural filter, absorbing and processing pollutants that flow into the park.

The water source for this swamp is groundwater that seeps from the edge of the bluff into the lower-lying area. This groundwater has been accumulating in the 600-foot-thick sand layer beneath the muck swamp for millions of years. The acidic nature of the muck helps to break down pollutants into less harmful substances, contributing to the purification of the floodplain water.

Additionally, the muck provides a fertile habitat for trees like sweetbay, American holly, and swamp tupelo, which are adapted to thrive in wetter conditions. This unique ecosystem plays a crucial role in maintaining the overall health of Congaree's environment.

As you continue your journey, you will transition out of the muck swamp and into slightly higher, drier areas dominated by laurel oak. Subsequently, you will encounter wetter soils again, where baldcypress and water tupelo are the predominant tree species.

Site 3: Bald Cypress

Congaree National Park is renowned for its towering bald cypress trees, some of which are among the largest specimens in the entire nation. These ancient giants can live for over a millennium, reaching heights of 100 to 120 feet on average. Though they thrive in the wet environments like Congaree, bald cypress can also adapt to drier conditions. Their early leaf shedding earned them the nickname "bald."

Native to the southeastern United States and the Gulf Coastal Plains, bald cypress trees exhibit unique characteristics. As young saplings, their feathery leaves sprout directly from the trunk rather than branches. One of their most distinctive features is the presence of "knees," vertical protrusions that emerge from their root systems. These knees, though their exact purpose is still debated, provide structural support and may also help supply oxygen to roots during periods of flooding.

Known for its durability, bald cypress wood has been aptly called "the wood eternal." Native Americans valued it for making canoes, while early European settlers used it to construct shingles, siding, docks, and other structures. Unfortunately, extensive logging in the 19th century decimated many bald cypress forests, making the trees in Congaree National Park a precious remnant of old-growth stands in the United States.

Site 4: Water Tupelo

Interspersed with the majestic bald cypress are water tupelo trees, which also thrive in wet environments. While both species have swollen trunks, they can be distinguished by their leaf shapes and root systems. Bald cypress often grows straight and tall, while water tupelo trunks are more sinuous. Additionally, bald cypress leaves are thin and needle-like, whereas water tupelo possess broader, flat, and smooth leaves. Both trees are well-adapted to floodplain environments, with water tupelo being more susceptible to crown damage during storms.

The Importance of Old Growth Forests

An old growth forest is one that has grown undisturbed for a significant period. These forests are characterized by high species diversity, multiple habitats, and trees of mixed age. In this specific area of the park, downed logs and standing snags provide unique habitats, and the trees form a patchy canopy layer. This uneven sunlight distribution creates a diverse understory, supporting plants like dwarf palmetto and American holly that thrive in a mix of sun and shade.

The uneven sunlight distribution also allows plants to begin their life cycles at different times, resulting in a mixed age forest. This creates a more stable ecosystem, as trees of the same species and age are less likely to die concurrently. Uniform forests, on the other hand, tend to be less stable due to the potential for frequent succession events.

Site 5: Switch Cane and European Settlement

Similar in appearance to bamboo, the tall, reedy plant seen here is known as switch cane, an Arundinaria species. Switch cane favors shady growing conditions, damp soil or seepage habitats, and slightly elevated locations, which are found in abundance within the park. As such, switch cane has largely taken over the area and formed what is known as a canebrake, or a thicket of switch cane.

Historical Significance

Prior to European settlement in the southeastern United States, switch cane was widely prevalent and an important resource for Native Americans. They incorporated this versatile plant into their everyday life as medicine, building materials, weapons, baskets, adornments, and musical instruments. Native Americans conducted prescribed burns, which maintained ideal, moderate disturbance conditions. These burns eliminated woodier vegetation as major competitors, and provided ideal conditions for switch cane to thrive.

Decline and Conservation

Switch cane was also valuable to settlers since it provided an abundant and rapidly growing source of food for livestock. Canebrakes indicated fertile soil, so surrounding land became popular areas to settle. Overgrazing, inconsistent burn practices, and land development led to a major decline in canebrake communities over time. Today, large canebrakes no longer exist outside of preserved areas like Congaree National Park, due to greater disturbance than switch cane can handle.

Site 6: Snags and Wildlife

Snags, or standing dead trees, are a common sight in Congaree National Park. These remnants of once-living trees play a crucial role in the park's ecosystem. They are often the result of environmental stressors such as lightning, high winds, wildfires, ice storms, drought, disease, or simply old age. Over time, the bark peels away, and the tree begins to deteriorate.

Despite their lifeless appearance, snags serve as a vital habitat for a variety of organisms. Fungi and bacteria find a suitable host and food source in the decaying wood. Insects like the patent leather beetle live, feed, and lay eggs in the decaying trunk. Birds, unable to create their own nest cavities, rely on snags for natural nesting sites. Woodpeckers, such as the pileated woodpecker, often excavate cavities in these dead trees, providing homes for themselves and other birds.

Snags also benefit larger predators. Owls, ospreys, and woodpeckers use snags as perching or hunting posts. The exposed roots of downed trees can serve as small perches or nesting sites for smaller animals. Additionally, many species store food within the trunks of snags.

In conclusion, snags are not merely remnants of the past but essential components of the Congaree National Park ecosystem. They provide habitat for a diverse range of organisms, from fungi and insects to birds and mammals. By understanding the ecological importance of snags, we can appreciate their role in maintaining the park's biodiversity.

Site 7: Logging

In the early and mid-19th century, the rapid industrialization of the United States led to a surge in demand for timber. Vast tracts of old-growth forests in the northeast and upper midwest were cleared to support infrastructure development, including the construction of towns, railroads, and factories. As resources in these regions dwindled, attention turned to the south, where industrialization had been slower to develop and untouched forests still remained.

Francis Beidler, a timber mogul from Chicago, capitalized on this opportunity. In the early 1900s, he purchased over 140,000 acres of land in South Carolina, intending to exploit the prized bald cypress trees found there. Beidler established the Santee River Cypress Lumber Company and began logging operations. However, he soon encountered significant challenges. The bald cypress trees, known for their durability and resistance to rot, proved to be difficult to cut down and transport. Many freshly-felled trees were simply too heavy to float down the Congaree River, leading to substantial losses. Loggers eventually learned to girdle the trees and let them dry for a year before harvesting.

Despite these difficulties, logging remained economically impractical. Francis Beidler ultimately decided to halt operations and preserve his land as a timber reserve. While millions of acres of southern old-growth bottomland hardwoods were logged during this period, Beidler's tracts remained largely untouched. His decision was motivated by the belief that timber prices would rise in the future, making his land more valuable.

Beidler's land remained in timber reserve status until 1969, when his heirs attempted to resume logging in response to high demand for timber. However, their plans were met with opposition from conservationists who recognized the ecological significance of the area. Ultimately, a portion of Beidler's land was preserved as Congaree National Park, a protected area that showcases the beauty and biodiversity of old-growth bottomland hardwood forests. Beidler's unintended legacy has helped to safeguard a valuable natural resource for future generations.

Site 11: Loblolly Pines and Champion Trees

Congaree National Park is known for its bottomland hardwood forest, but it also harbors a surprising element: pine trees. While many pine species struggle to survive in wetland conditions, the loblolly pine thrives in such environments. Its name, "loblolly," aptly describes its preference for muddy areas.

The loblolly pine is a vital part of the park's ecosystem. It provides homes for various bird species and offers food for small rodents. Additionally, its rapid growth makes it a valuable source of lumber. These trees can reach heights of 50 to 80 feet, but in Congaree National Park, they can grow even taller. In fact, the park is home to the tallest known loblolly pine in the world, standing at an impressive 169 feet.

Congaree National Park is a treasure trove of champion trees, those with exceptional size or age. The American Forests organization has established the National Big Tree Program to recognize and protect these remarkable specimens. To qualify as a champion, a tree must be native to or naturalized in the continental United States and meet specific size criteria. Congaree boasts a high concentration of champion trees, including the loblolly pine, sweetgum, laurel oak, American elm, Shumard oak, and others.

One particularly notable tree in Congaree is the Richland County Pine. Dating back to the 1750s, this tree provides a glimpse into the park's history, predating the establishment of Richland County itself.

Site 12: Weston Lake

A natural body of water, Weston Lake holds significant ecological value within the park. Originally a small bend in the Congaree River, it has evolved over time into an oxbow lake. Oxbow lakes are named for their distinctive U-shaped form, created by the erosion and deposition processes that occur along river banks.

As water flows more slowly along the inner bend of a river, sediments are deposited, gradually narrowing the bend. Conversely, water moves faster along the outer bend, eroding the riverbank. Eventually, the bend becomes so narrow that it separates from the main river, forming the characteristic oxbow shape.

Weston Lake is a haven for a diverse array of aquatic life, including amphibians, fish, and reptiles. Along its banks, visitors may encounter snapping turtles, yellow-bellied sliders, and other species of freshwater turtles. The lake also serves as a habitat for various fish species, such as gar and sunfish.

Site 14: Dwarf Palmetto

Near this marker is an abundance of dwarf palmetto, an undergrowth plant with numerous fronds that resemble a fan. Dwarf palmetto are common in the southern and central U.S. and can withstand short periods of extremely cold temperatures, despite residing in a mild climate.

The abundance of dwarf palmetto can be attributed to a few factors, including the disturbance caused by Hurricane Hugo, the deadliest and costliest hurricane to have hit South Carolina. Landing in 1989 as a category 4 storm, Hurricane Hugo primarily affected the South Carolina low country, near Charleston and Myrtle Beach. However, extremely strong winds, up to 90 mph inland, brought damage throughout the state. In the park, Hugo toppled two champion trees, a Shumard oak and an overcup oak, and it is estimated that 60% of the largest trees sustained damage.

The wind damage sustained by these large trees thinned the dense canopy layer, allowing enough sunlight for shade intolerant species to populate the forests. As such, smaller trees like sweetgum and oak saplings, and undergrowth plants like the dwarf palmetto have had the opportunity to thrive in this area. Large storms like Hurricane Hugo allow for forest renewal via succession, or a prolonged period of change in the species diversity, abundance, and distribution within an ecological community.

Site 15: Old Still Site

In the heart of the Congaree National Park, amidst the towering trees and lush undergrowth, lies a relic of a bygone era. Between the boardwalk, partially obscured by vegetation, is a large, old iron portion of a still, roughly 20 to 30 feet from the path. This apparatus, used to distill liquids through boiling and condensation, once served a clandestine purpose: moonshining.

The Prohibition era, a period of nationwide alcohol prohibition in the United States, saw a surge in illegal liquor production. Driven by religious and feminist motivations, Prohibition sparked widespread controversy. While the law aimed to curb alcohol consumption, it also fueled a thriving black market, leading to the rise of moonshiners and bootleggers.

In South Carolina, the Prohibition movement was marked by class tensions. As one local put it, "a rich family could have a cellar-full of liquor and get by, it seemed, but if a poor family had one bottle of home-brew, there would be trouble." To address the issue, the state implemented a dispensary system, regulating alcohol sales through state-run facilities. However, despite these efforts, illegal moonshining remained a common practice.

The Congaree floodplain, with its dense vegetation, remote location, and ample water resources, provided an ideal hiding place for moonshiners and their stills. Scattered throughout the park, one can find abandoned still sites in various states of decay. These remnants serve as a testament to the illicit activities that once took place within these secluded woodlands.

Site 18: Harry Hampton

Harry Hampton, a local reporter, editor, and avid outdoorsman, played a pivotal role in preserving the Congaree floodplain for future generations. A native of Columbia, South Carolina, Hampton's passion for wildlife and conservation led him to advocate for the protection of the Beidler Tract, a vast expanse of bottomland hardwood forest. His journey began with a simple hobby: hunting.

After frequenting the Beidler Tract, Hampton recognized its unique ecological value, characterized by its diverse species and towering trees. Impressed by the floodplain's significance, he embarked on a mission to safeguard this natural treasure. However, his initial lobbying efforts faced resistance from those opposed to creating a national park.

A turning point came in 1969 when the Beidler family announced plans to resume logging operations on the tract. Conservationists, inspired by Hampton's vision, rallied behind the Congaree Swamp National Preserve Association and intensified their lobbying campaign. Their persistence paid off, and in 1976, the Congaree Swamp National Monument was established.

While the Beidlers managed to log approximately 2500 acres before federal protection took effect, they eventually sold their remaining land to the government for a substantial sum. The establishment of the monument marked a significant victory for conservation efforts, preserving a vital piece of old-growth bottomland forest.

Congaree National Park, as it became in 2003, stands as a testament to Hampton's legacy. Despite the widespread loss of old-growth bottomland forests in the southeastern United States, Congaree remains the largest such forest in America. Its designation as a national park has brought increased recognition and resources, fostering efforts to enhance its visibility and outreach.

Site 19: Freedmen and Slaves

The trail marker stands amidst a tapestry of nature, surrounded by undergrowth, trees, and shrubs. Among the flora, a fallen loblolly pine, sweetgum, and holly tree lie, their twisted roots and natural debris forming a rugged landscape. This dense vegetation, coupled with the thick muck, created a challenging terrain for slave owners and slave catchers to navigate. It offered runaway slaves a place of concealment, leading to the establishment of settlements in the river floodplains and the birth of communities within the forest. Congaree Park became a haven for those fleeing slavery, a temporary refuge for both slaves on the run and freedmen seeking to avoid recapture.

Charles Ball and Jacob Stroyer, two notable figures, documented their harrowing experiences as slaves in the Congaree region. Ball, in his autobiography "The Life and Adventures of Charles Ball," detailed his time on a plantation along the Congaree River. Stroyer, in his work "My Life in the South," recounted his life as a slave at Headquarters Plantation, near the eastern end of the park. Their accounts provide invaluable insights into the struggles and resilience of enslaved individuals seeking freedom.

In the 20th century, the history of African Americans in Congaree Park was further explored and documented. Edward C.L. Adams, a local white physician, collected and recorded the stories of African Americans in the area. His compilation, "Tales of the Congaree," offers a glimpse into the lives, experiences, and perspectives of the African-American community. These stories, told in the vernacular of the time, include supernatural tales, encounters with wildlife, and accounts of the hardships faced during the era of lynchings and Jim Crow laws.

Site 20: African Americans of Lower Richlands

Today, Congaree National Park stands as a testament to the enduring spirit of its African American residents. The park's history is deeply intertwined with the struggles and triumphs of the enslaved people who once called this land home. One such landmark, the Harriet Barber House, serves as a poignant reminder of the resilience and determination of African Americans in the face of adversity.

Following the abolition of slavery, Harriet and Samuel Barber, two former slaves, purchased a 42.5-acre tract of land in 1872 through the South Carolina Land Commission. This groundbreaking program aimed to provide freedmen with the opportunity to own their own land. While many African Americans participated in the program, the Barbers were one of the few families to retain their property. The Harriet Barber House, now listed on the National Register of Historic Places, stands as a symbol of their perseverance and the lasting legacy they left behind.

The Southeast Rural Community Outreach (SERCO) has been instrumental in preserving and promoting the history of Lower Richland and its African American residents. In partnership with Mount Moriah Baptist Church and Congaree National Park, SERCO hosts Swampfest each fall, a cultural festival that celebrates the region's heritage. The festival features nature walks, educational talks, and other activities that highlight the communities that historically inhabited the park, including maroons, runaway slaves, and Native Americans.

Through public outreach initiatives and historically significant sites like the Harriet Barber House, Congaree National Park continues to honor the rich and complex history of its African American community. These efforts serve as a reminder of the enduring spirit of resilience and the enduring legacy of those who have shaped the park's cultural landscape.

Difficulty:

The trail is rated easy, making it suitable for hikers of all ages and abilities.

Type of hike:

The trail is a loop, so you'll return to your starting point after completing the hike.

Dogs are allowed on the trail, but they must be leashed at all times

The trail is family-friendly and suitable for kids of all ages

Length:

The trail is 2.4 miles long.

Estimated time to complete:

The average estimated time to complete the trail is 1-2 hours.

Accessibility:

The trail is accessible for visitors using wheelchairs, mobility equipment, or strollers. There are 2 designated van-accessible parking spaces in the paved parking lot.

Trailhead Elevation: 105 feet

Total Elevation Gain: Minimal

Highest Elevation: 115 feet

Ability:

The trail is suitable for hikers of all ages and abilities.

Features:

The trail offers stunning views of the old-growth forest, including towering trees, cypress knees, and Weston Lake. It's a great place to spot wildlife, such as turtles, birds, and deer.

Allowed uses:

The trail is open to hiking only.

Trail surface:

The trail is made of wood, providing a smooth and stable surface.

Best time to hike:

The trail can be hiked year-round, but the spring and fall are the most pleasant times to visit. Spring is a great time to see wildflowers, while fall offers beautiful fall foliage.

Boardwalk Trail

Tips

Take Your Time: The Boardwalk Loop Trail is a great opportunity to relax and enjoy the natural beauty of the park. Don't feel rushed to finish the trail quickly.

Look Up: The towering trees in Congaree National Park are truly impressive. Take a moment to look up and appreciate their size and beauty.

Listen: Pay attention to the sounds of the forest. You might hear birds singing, frogs croaking, or squirrels chattering.

Bluff Trail

Trailhead: The Bluff Trail begins at the Harry Hampton Visitor Center in Congaree National Park.

Description:

The Bluff Trail Network offers a delightful one-hour walk along a 2.0-mile loop trail, with additional spur trails leading to campgrounds and a connector trail accessible from the Harry Hampton Visitor Center parking lot. This trail system, comprised of the Longleaf Trail (#8), Bluff Trail (#1), and Firefly Trail (#10), is located just beyond the crossing of the entrance road and provides access to both the Longleaf and Bluff campgrounds.

As you explore the trails, you'll be immersed in the unique scenery and cultural history of the area. The trails also offer a glimpse into the park's efforts to establish a longleaf pine savanna habitat through controlled burns. Keep your eyes peeled for wildlife sightings, including deer, box turtles, and fox squirrels. Listen for the calls of red-headed woodpeckers, brown-headed nuthatches, and pine warblers, which can be heard year-round. During the summer, you may also encounter eastern wood-pewees, Kentucky warblers, and yellow-throated vireos.

One of the park's most popular attractions is the annual firefly display in May. This synchronized light show is a rare occurrence in the eastern US, and the park manages visitor interest through a reservation system to ensure a memorable experience along the Firefly Trail.

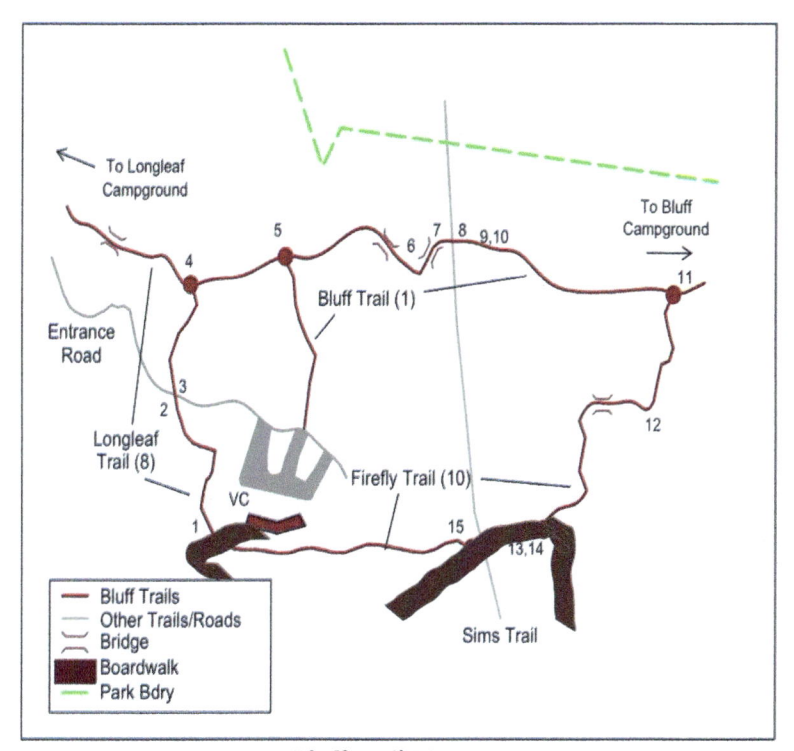

Bluff Trail Map

Site 1: Accessing the Trails

To embark on your journey along the Longleaf Trail, begin by entering the Harry Hampton Visitor Center. Once inside, follow the breezeway to the boardwalk. Walk along the boardwalk for a short distance until you notice a set of stairs on your right, positioned in front of a large beech tree. These stairs lead down to the Longleaf Trail.

Finding the Trailhead

As you descend the stairs, locate the trail sign directly ahead. Turn left and follow the Longleaf Trail to commence your hike. To ensure you're on the correct path, keep an eye out for the white signs marked with the number eight that are posted on trees along the trail.

Reaching the Entrance Road

The walk from the boardwalk to the entrance road of Congaree National Park is brief, taking only a couple of minutes. So, relax and enjoy the natural beauty that surrounds you as you venture into this enchanting park.

Site 2: Entrance Road

In the 1990s, Congaree National Park sought to increase its annual visitor count. To achieve this goal, the park decided to construct a new entrance road and a visitor center. The new road would replace the privately-held Caroline Sims Road, which had previously served as the park's entrance.

Funding Challenges and a Partnership

The park initially requested $5.8 million from the National Park Service to fund the construction of the new road and visitor center. However, this proposal was unfortunately denied. Faced with this setback, the park explored alternative methods to complete the projects.

To reduce the overall construction costs, the park formed an unprecedented partnership with the River Alliance, Richland County, and the S.C. National Guard. This collaboration served as a model for other national parks, as federal projects often require significant time commitments from the National Guard and are typically larger in scale.

Military Involvement

The official roster for the entrance road project included troops from the S.C. Army and Air National Guard, as well as civil engineering squadrons from as far away as Ohio and Pennsylvania. Their involvement played a crucial role in the successful completion of the project.

Site 3: Controlled Burn

As you enter the park, you'll immediately notice a fascinating blend of vegetation. The understory is dominated by young sweetgum saplings, while towering loblolly pine trees form the canopy. You might also spot charred bark near the base of some trees or fallen limbs with signs of fire damage. These seemingly unrelated features are actually connected by a carefully planned intervention.

The park regularly conducts controlled burns, which have covered much of the area surrounding the Bluff Trail. These controlled fires serve a crucial purpose: to limit the spread of sweetgum and create an open understory that longleaf pines favor. Longleaf pine habitats once spanned an impressive 70 million acres across the Southeast, supporting a rich array of plant and animal life, including the endangered Red-cockaded Woodpecker. By restoring these habitats through controlled burns, the park aims to encourage the reintroduction of this iconic bird species.

Site 4: Longleaf Campground

As you venture further into the park, you'll encounter a trail fork. To the left lies the continuation of the Longleaf Trail, leading you directly to the Longleaf Campground. If you're eager to explore the campground, you can either follow the spur trail on foot or drive there via the entrance road, which you might recall passing on your way in.

Choosing the right path will lead you to the Bluff Trail, marked by distinctive white number one signs on the trees. Embarking on this trail will unveil the park's scenic beauty and unique features.

Site 5: Land Use History

As you continue your journey east along the Bluff Trail, you'll come across a connecting trail on your right, marked with the number #1. This trail offers a shortcut back to the parking lot if you wish to shorten your hike.

Walking along the Bluff Trail, you'll notice man-made ditches lining the sides of the path. To help you cross these ditches, there are a few bridges strategically placed along the trail. These structures serve as reminders of the area's past and the human impact on the landscape.

Aerial photographs from 1938 reveal that the land surrounding the Bluff Trail was once cultivated farmland, devoid of trees. The man-made ditches you see today were created to drain wetlands and prepare the land for agriculture. Research conducted by Neal Polhemus has uncovered the history behind these ditches. One of the landowners was Reverend Daniel Boyd and his wife Amanda, who had previously been enslaved on the Bluff property. Reverend Boyd was a pastor at several local churches, including St. Mark Baptist, New Light Beulah Baptist, and Mt. Moriah Baptist. In 1873, Robert Adams sold an 87-acre tract of land to Reverend Boyd, and Amanda continued to live there after her husband's passing. The shallow ditches you encounter today are remnants of this historical period and the cultural significance of the area.

While Congaree National Park is generally known for its ancient bottomland forests, the forest along the Bluff Trail is relatively young. It's fascinating to imagine that the trail you're walking on was once a cleared field, surrounded by open farmland just a few decades ago.

Site 6: From Loblolly to Longleaf

As you venture further along the trail, the characteristics of a fire-maintained longleaf pine habitat become increasingly evident. The foliage begins to showcase greater diversity, a hallmark of longleaf savanna ecosystems. This harmonious blend of tall pines and a rich variety of understory vegetation is a common sight in this environment.

Just beyond the Caroline Sims Road intersection, the contrast in plant diversity becomes even more pronounced. You might start encountering plants like beautyberry, winged sumac, and an expanded range of grasses earlier in your journey. Beautyberry bushes are distinguished by their large oval leaves and attractive clusters of deep purple berries. Winged sumac, a smaller plant, features compound leaves that transform into a vibrant red color during late fall. These plants serve as early indicators of the upcoming shift in foliage, signaling the transition into the diverse longleaf pine habitat.

Site 7: Caroline Sims Road

Caroline Sims Road, once a vital gateway to Congaree National Park, has undergone a significant transformation. Prior to the construction of the park's new entrance road, this route served as the primary access point. However, in recent years, the lower portion of Caroline Sims Road has been renamed Sims Trail, a tribute to Booker T Sims, a local resident who played a crucial role in the park's early development.

Sims, who resided nearby on Old Bluff Road, generously volunteered his carpentry skills to assist in the park's construction and maintenance. While he sadly passed away in 2002, his former house remains a visible landmark just east of the park entrance.

The road crossing at Caroline Sims Road offers a striking contrast between the initial landscape and the park's current ecological goals. Upon crossing the current entrance road, visitors are greeted by a predominantly sweet gum and loblolly pine-dominated environment. However, as one proceeds further along Caroline Sims Road, a more ideal longleaf savanna habitat emerges.

Until a recent pine bark beetle infestation, the area immediately following the road crossing served as an excellent example of the park's efforts to restore and maintain longleaf savanna through controlled burns. These controlled burns are essential for promoting the growth of fire-adapted species like longleaf pine and reducing the risk of destructive wildfires.

Site 8: Old Whiskey Still

Off Caroline Sims Road to your left lies one of Congaree National Park's largest historic moonshine still sites. The site is most visible during the winter or after a controlled burn, marked by two large, rusted steel boilers. Scattered around these boilers are several 55-gallon drums and numerous broken Mason jars.

This moonshine operation is believed to have been active throughout the 20th century, continuing until the 1970s. Authorities likely discovered and dismantled the site by detonating the boilers under pressure and using axes to destroy the remaining metal drums. Hidden along the bluff edge and within the muck swamp are numerous smaller still sites, remnants of the region's illicit moonshining past.

Site 9: Pine Bark Beetles

As you continue along the Bluff trail, you'll encounter a large clearing. This open space is a consequence of efforts to combat the pine bark beetle infestation, a significant threat to the establishment of a longleaf savanna habitat in this region.

Pine bark beetles bore into the bark of trees, feeding and laying eggs. Their larvae consume the tree's nutrients, eventually killing it. Once a tree dies, adult beetles move on to infect neighboring trees. To prevent the spread of beetles, infected trees were removed and nearby areas were cleared to create buffer zones. However, this approach proved ineffective as the infestation worsened in subsequent years.

Despite the challenges, this clearing aligns with the natural openings found in longleaf pine savannas, which can promote the growth of new pine seedlings.

It's important to note that pine bark beetles can be found in various locations, including national parks and even your own backyard. To detect an infestation, observe the color of the needles on nearby pine trees. If the needles turn from green to a lighter, rusty brown, it may indicate a pine bark beetle infestation.

Site 11: Bluff Campground

After clearing the initial section of the trail, you'll encounter a fork in the path. To reach Bluff Campground, head straight ahead on the short spur trail. If you prefer to continue on the loop trail, veer right onto the Firefly Trail, which is marked by white number ten signs.

Site 12: The Bluff Edge

As you venture away from the campsite and into the deeper woods, you'll find yourself approaching the edge of a bluff. This area is a unique ecological transition zone known as an ecotone. It serves as a bridge between the lush muck bottomland forest and the diverse bluff forest.

The bluff forest is renowned for its remarkable array of plant and animal life. This richness stems from its ability to incorporate elements from both neighboring ecosystems. It's a prime spot to observe fascinating creatures like the eastern box turtle as they navigate between the swamp and the higher ground.

As you continue your hike, keep your eyes peeled for intriguing critters making their way from one habitat to the next. Pay close attention to the vibrant tapestry of plant species that line the bluff's edge. In the springtime, you might encounter the intriguing jack-in-the-pulpit with its curious flower. And throughout the growing season, the stately vase-shaped cinnamon fern, with its distinctive cinnamon-colored fertile fronds, adds to the visual splendor.

Site 13: Armadillo Burrows

As you hike back to the boardwalk, you might notice some interesting features along the trail. There are several dirt mounds pushed up against the boardwalk, which are actually burrows. These burrows are home to armadillos, a fascinating creature that has been expanding its range northward in recent years.

The nine-banded armadillo, named for its distinctive shell composed of nine overlapping bands, is a unique mammal. It has a pig-like snout, is primarily nocturnal, and prefers habitats with dense shade and plenty of tree cover. These animals are known for their extensive burrowing habits, creating tunnels that can reach 7-8 inches in diameter and extend up to 15 feet long.

While armadillos are fascinating creatures, spotting one in the daytime can be quite difficult. They are most active at night, so if you're hoping to catch a glimpse of one, it might be best to return to the boardwalk after dark.

Site 14: Horse sugar Trees

Along the boardwalk, you'll encounter an intriguing plant called horse sugar. These trees, also known as sweet leaf, are located just past the armadillo burrows. Their leaves are a deep green, thick, and have a glossy sheen, although they are often affected by fleshy galls caused by a fungus. From March to May, these trees bloom with fragrant white flowers and thrive in damp, shaded woodlands.

One of the interesting aspects of horse sugar trees is their taste! Chewing the leaves reveals a flavor reminiscent of a green apple. In the past, local landowners would let their livestock graze in the swamp during the summer, and horse sugar trees were a popular choice for the animals to browse.

Site 15: Second Sims Trail Crossing

Perpendicular to the boardwalk is Sims Trail. Once the main entryway to the park, this gravel road now serves as both a trail and service road. It leads from the bluff down to Cedar Creek and Wise Lake.

Beyond Sims Trail, a portion of the Firefly Trail is used for the annual firefly program. These synchronized fireflies are male Photinus frontalis beetles, who signal to females as part of a display. The females on the ground signal back, though their signaling is less understood. Initial displays are not perfectly synchronized, so visitors cannot be guaranteed a fully synchronized show. However, they will still see fireflies and enjoy a peaceful evening in the park.

To return to the Visitor Center, continue along the boardwalk or take the Firefly Trail through a beautiful oak-beech forest.

Difficulty: Easy

Type of Hike: Loop

Dogs are allowed but must be on a leash

This trail is suitable for children

Length: 2.1 miles

Estimated Time to Complete: 1 hour

Accessibility: The trail is mostly accessible, with a portion of it being a boardwalk. However, there are some stairs and uneven terrain.

Trailhead Elevation: Approximately 100 feet

Total Elevation Gain: Minimal

Highest Elevation: Around 120 feet

Ability: Suitable for most people, including families and those new to hiking.

Features: The Bluff Trail offers a peaceful forest setting and opportunities to observe local wildlife.

Allowed Uses: Hiking

Trail Surface: Mostly dirt and boardwalk.

Best Time to Hike: The Bluff Trail can be enjoyed year-round, but spring and fall offer pleasant weather and fewer crowds.

Note: While the Bluff Trail is a relatively easy hike, it's still important to wear appropriate footwear and bring plenty of water, especially during warmer months.

Sims Trail

Trailhead: Harry Hampton Visitor Center, Congaree National Park

Description:

The Sims Trail, a 2.1-mile-long path, winds through the heart of Congaree National Park. Named after a local volunteer, Booker T. Sims, this trail offers a unique opportunity to explore the park's diverse ecosystem.

Originally an old road leading to a hunt club lodge, the Sims Trail now serves as a scenic alternative to the park's longer hiking trails. It's particularly popular among families due to its wide path and shallow puddles that attract a variety of wildlife.

As you traverse the trail, you'll encounter towering loblolly pines, a hallmark of the park's preservation efforts. Dead trees, or snags, provide habitats for woodpeckers and other birds. The trail also passes through wetlands, offering excellent opportunities for wildlife observation.

To reach the Sims Trail, you can follow the boardwalk from the Visitor Center or take the Bluff Trail. The trail is well-marked with numbered signs, making it easy to navigate. However, keep in mind that the park is a wilderness area, so there are limited human-made features.

Whether you're a seasoned hiker or simply seeking a leisurely stroll, the Sims Trail offers a rewarding experience in the heart of Congaree National Park.

Parking

Visitor Center

Sims Trail

1
2
3
4
5

Weston Lake

6

7

- Sims Trail
- Other trail
- Bridge
- Boardwalk

Site 1: Start of Trail

The Sims Trail begins at its intersection with the Boardwalk. As you look uphill towards the north, you'll find the trail leads to the park's essential facilities, including maintenance, fire management, and research areas. Standing at the trail's edge, you're at the boundary between the park's uplands and the floodplain forest.

The uplands are managed through controlled burns every few years. These burns mimic both natural wildfires and the fire management practices of Native Americans, creating an open forest dominated by fire-resistant longleaf and loblolly pine trees. This habitat is ideal for various game animals, including deer, turkey, and bobwhite. Longleaf pine savannah once covered a vast area of the southeastern United States, supporting endangered species like the Red-cockaded Woodpecker and Bachman's Sparrow. Conservation efforts have helped increase the extent of this biologically rich ecosystem, though it still remains a fraction of its former range.

Turning right onto the Sims Trail, you'll pass through a narrow band of muck or peat swamp. A thick layer of peat, accumulated since the last Ice Age, filters groundwater entering the park from the bluff edge. The swamp's characteristic trees include a canopy of Swamp Tupelo and American Holly, with a midstory of Red Bay and Sweet Bay and an understory of Doghobble, Cinnamon Fern, and sedge.

Site 2: Loblolly Pine

As you venture down Sims Trail in Congaree National Park, you'll be greeted by an unexpected sight: towering stands of Loblolly Pine trees. These tall, slender trees are unusual in this bottomland hardwood forest, as many pine species struggle to survive in wetland environments. However, the Loblolly Pine is uniquely adapted to thrive in these wet conditions, with its name literally meaning "muddy puddle."

These pines are among the tallest trees you'll encounter in the park, often reaching heights of 50 to 80 feet. In fact, the world's tallest known Loblolly Pine stands proudly within Congaree National Park, reaching an impressive 169 feet.

The Impact of Hurricane Hugo

Hurricane Hugo, which devastated the region in 1989, left its mark on the Loblolly Pine stands in this part of the park. Longtime visitors often comment on the beautiful pine groves that once shaded the undergrowth of Switchcane along the Sims Trail. Switchcane, a plant similar in appearance to bamboo, thrives in shady conditions, damp soil, and slightly elevated floodplain locations. Dense stands of Switchcane, known as canebrakes, provide critical nesting habitat for several bottomland bird species, including the Swainson's warbler.

The Importance of Snags

Throughout the park, you'll also notice snags—standing dead trees—and tip-ups, fallen trees with uprooted root systems. Snags are caused by various environmental factors, such as lightning, high winds, wildfires, ice storms, drought, disease, and old age. While dead, these trees play a vital role in the ecosystem.

Snags serve as crucial habitat for fungi, bacteria, insects, and small animals. Fungi and bacteria decompose the decaying tree, providing food and a host. Insects like the patent leather beetle live, feed, and lay eggs in the decaying trunk. Birds that lack the ability to create their own nest cavities often rely on snags for natural nesting sites. Larger hunting birds like owls, raptors, and woodpeckers use snags as perching or hunting posts. Even the exposed roots of downed trees can provide shelter and nesting sites for small animals.

Snags are essential for maintaining the biodiversity of Congaree National Park, demonstrating the interconnectedness of all living things in this unique ecosystem.

Site 3: Dwarf Palmetto

Near this marker, you'll find a thriving population of Dwarf Palmetto, a fan-leaved undergrowth plant common in the southern and central United States. Despite their preference for mild climates, these resilient plants can tolerate short periods of extreme cold. The abundance of Dwarf Palmetto here is closely tied to the edge of a former stream's sediment deposit.

Hurricane Hugo played a significant role in the flourishing of these plants. The storm's powerful winds thinned the dense canopy, allowing more sunlight to reach the forest floor. This increased sunlight provided an opportunity for shade-intolerant species, such as sweetgum and oak saplings, to establish themselves. Dwarf Palmetto, as an undergrowth plant, also benefited from this increased light availability.

Large storms like Hurricane Hugo can act as catalysts for forest renewal. The process of succession, a gradual change in species diversity, abundance, and distribution within an ecological community, is often triggered by such events. By creating openings in the canopy, hurricanes allow new species to colonize the area and contribute to the overall health and resilience of the forest.

Site 4: Moccasin Alley

As you venture towards the bridge at Moccasin Alley, you'll notice the lasting impacts of natural disasters. An ice storm in 2014 and Hurricane Matthew in 2016 have left their mark, creating gaps in the canopy and uprooting trees. Despite the damage, nature's resilience is evident. The alley's numerous puddles attract a variety of wildlife, from dragonflies and butterflies to birds seeking a cool bath. Keep an eye out for the vibrant Six-spotted Tiger Beetle, its iridescent green wings adorned with subtle white spots.

A Haven for Wildlife

Moccasin Alley serves as a vital waterway, connecting upstream wetlands to Weston Lake. This environment provides ideal conditions for predatory birds like the Red-shouldered Hawk and Barred Owl. In the summer, the alley is a hotspot for the golden Prothonotary Warbler and offers opportunities to observe frogs and snakes. However, it's important to remember the alley's namesake: the Water Moccasin. These venomous snakes can be encountered here, along with other watersnakes seeking food or shelter.

A Resilient Structure

The sturdy bridge at Moccasin Alley stands as a testament to the park's experience with frequent flooding. The Congaree River's expansive watershed, stretching into North Carolina, contributes to the park's vulnerability to floodwaters. The bridge's design, with its system of anchors and stays, reflects the lessons learned from past floods, ensuring its durability in the face of nature's challenges.

Site 5: Boardwalk Loop Trail Crossing

The Sims Trail and Boardwalk Trail offer a scenic hiking experience in Weston State Park. The Sims Trail intersects the Boardwalk shortly after crossing the bridge over Moccasin Gut. Here, hikers have the option to shorten their hike by turning right onto the Low Boardwalk and following the signs back to the Visitor Center.

For those who want to continue exploring, turning left on the Boardwalk Trail leads to several highlights. Just 150 yards away stands the massive Richland County Pine, an impressive landmark. Another 150 yards further, hikers will reach the Weston Lake overlook, a perfect spot to rest and enjoy the view.

From the overlook, hikers can retrace their steps back to the Sims Trail and continue their journey, or they can choose to return to the Visitor Center via the elevated portion of the Boardwalk Loop Trail.

Site 6: Weston Gut

The trail crosses Weston Gut, a small, short floodplain stream that plays a crucial role in the Congaree National Park's ecosystem. Known locally as a "gut," this waterway directs overflow from Cedar Creek into Weston Lake slough. Guts are distinguished from creeks by their shallower depth and shorter length. They often dry up or become stagnant during the summer and early fall. While they may seem to meander aimlessly across the floodplain, guts are essential for flood control. They transport water from the Congaree River throughout the floodplain during the initial stages of a flood and then channel it back to the river and main creeks as the flooding subsides.

The Baldcypress: A Symbol of the Southern Wetlands

The park is home to several tree species uniquely adapted to the wettest habitats in the floodplain. Among these, the Baldcypress is particularly dominant. This iconic tree is renowned for its straight trunk, feathery needles, and numerous "knees" that protrude from the water. Baldcypress decays slowly, earning it the nickname "the wood eternal." Historically, this wood was highly prized for shingles used in roofing and siding. Unfortunately, intense logging in the late 19th and early 20th centuries decimated many bald cypress forests in the southeastern United States. As a result, the Congaree National Park now boasts some of the last remaining old-growth bald cypress trees in the country.

Hunt Club Clearing

The trail opens up to the site of the former Cedar Creek Hunt Club cabin, a raised structure that once stood to the right. Other hunt club structures were also located in this clearing. The cabin replaced an earlier structure built by the United States Hunt Club, a name chosen to deter poaching.

Open areas like this are common throughout the park, having served as former feed plots for game, logging decks, or agricultural fields. Over time, these open spaces have evolved into "old field" habitats, characterized by fast-growing trees like Sweetgum and Loblolly Pine competing with blackberries and grape vines. This old field is rapidly transitioning into a dense forest, making it difficult to recognize its former cleared state.

Take advantage of the open sky to spot soaring birds, such as Mississippi Kites in summer or Red-shouldered Hawks year-round.

At the hunt club clearing, the trail terminates at a set of trail junctions marked by a directional sign. To return via a different route, turn sharply right and follow the Weston Lake Loop Trail back to the Low Boardwalk. The Low Boardwalk can then be followed back to the Visitor Center.

Difficulty: Easy

Type of Hike: Out-and-back

Dogs on leash are allowed

It is suitable for families

Length: 3 miles

Estimated Time to Complete: 1-2 hours

Accessibility: The trail is generally accessible, but there are some uneven sections.

Trailhead Elevation: Approximately 50 feet

Total Elevation Gain: Minimal

Highest Elevation: Around 60 feet

Ability: Suitable for most hikers, including beginners and families.

Features: Scenic forest views, wetlands, historic sites, and potential wildlife sightings (e.g., birds, deer).

Allowed Uses: Hiking

Trail Surface: Mostly packed dirt with some gravel sections.

Best Time to Hike: Spring and fall are ideal due to pleasant temperatures and reduced humidity. However, the park is beautiful year-round.

Additional Notes: The Sims Trail offers a shorter alternative to the longer trails in Congaree National Park. It's a great option for those seeking a leisurely hike or want to explore the park's diverse habitats.

Tips

Follow the Trail Markers: The trail is well-marked with brown blazes. Pay attention to the markers to stay on the correct path.

Be Mindful of Poison Ivy: Poison ivy is common in the park. Learn to recognize it and avoid touching it.

Take Breaks: The trail is relatively flat but can be hot and humid. Take frequent breaks to rest and hydrate.

Bates Ferry Trail

Trailhead:

Located off US 601, a few miles south of its junction with SC-48/Bluff Road.

Description:

The Bates Ferry Trail, a relatively new addition to Congaree National Park, opened its doors in 2015, marking the first trail created in the park in a quarter-century. This trail follows a causeway across the floodplain that has been in use for a century, itself tracing the path of a roadway that dates back to the 18th century. As such, it represents a significant milestone in the history of transportation in the Midlands region.

The trail offers visitors a glimpse into the past, providing a unique opportunity to experience how people traveled before the advent of trains and automobiles. Beyond its historical significance, the Bates Ferry Trail is a haven for nature enthusiasts. Keep your eyes peeled for deer and feral hogs roaming the trail, and marvel at the diverse flora and fauna that characterize Congaree National Park. The dense vegetation provides excellent birding opportunities year-round, attracting a variety of species. Additionally, the trail offers a prime habitat for spiders and butterflies.

For a moment of tranquility, head to the low bluff overlooking the Congaree River, where you can relax and enjoy the scenic views. A side trip to one of the park's largest baldcypress trees is also worth the effort.

A word of caution: The Bates Ferry Trail, like much of the park, is prone to flooding. Before embarking on your journey, be mindful of recent rainfall and water levels. If conditions are unfavorable, crossing the trail can be dangerous. Avoid deep flowing water and never hike alone in hazardous conditions. Always prioritize safety and exercise caution.

The Bates Ferry Trail is a well-marked path that leads you to the historic Bates Ferry landing. While the trail is wide and easy to follow, brown posts with the number "7" are strategically placed to guide hikers. These posts also provide GPS coordinates for emergency assistance.

This trail offers a glimpse into the natural beauty of the park. As you explore, you'll notice various numbered sites along the path. These sites correspond to significant natural or man-made features. Keep in mind that due to the wilderness designation, there are no signs or other human-made markers to indicate specific locations. The numbering on the map provides an approximate guide.

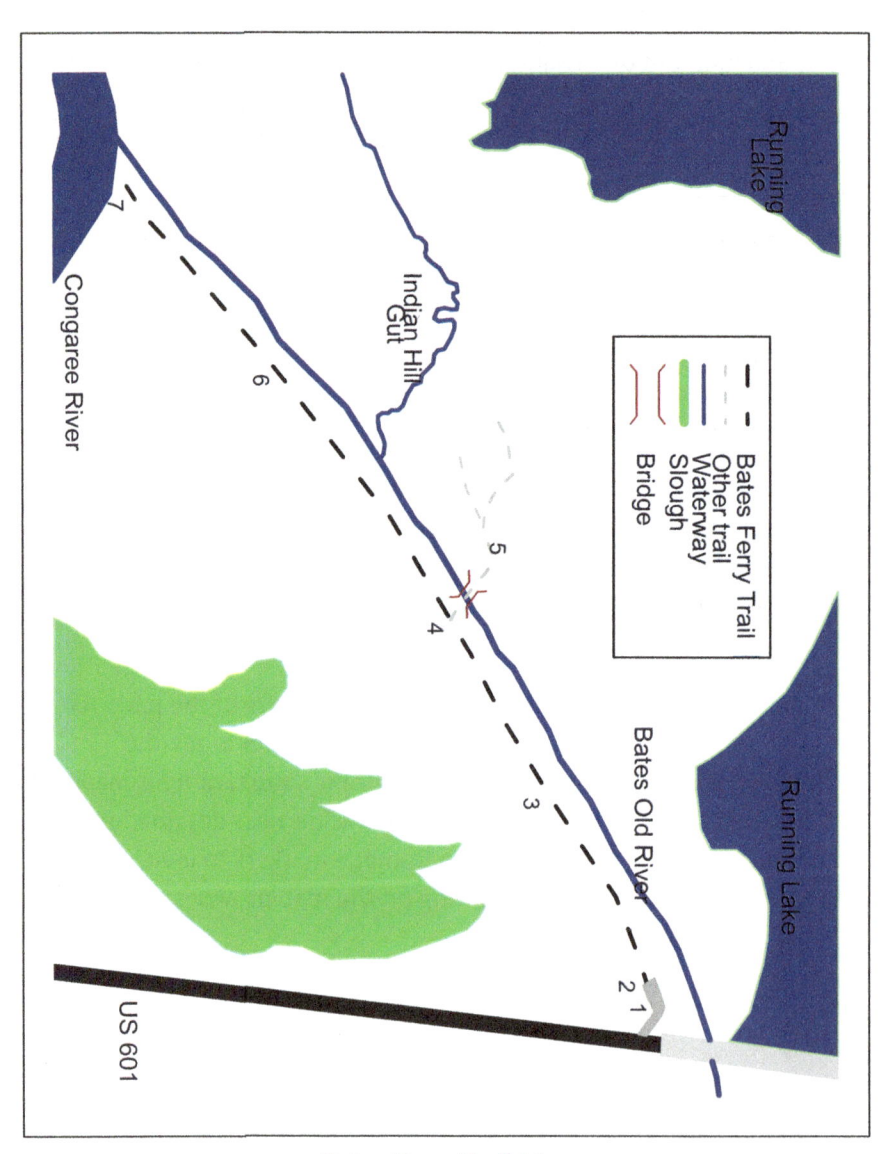

Bates Ferry Trail Map

Site 1: Entrance Kiosk

As you approach the Bates Ferry Trailhead, you'll be greeted by a historical kiosk to your left. This informative display provides valuable context for the trail, commemorating the history of Bates Ferry and the ferry system that once served the region. The kiosk recounts the historical route connecting Camden and Charleston, the extensive ferry system used to cross the Congaree River, and the eventual decline of ferries due to the advent of railroads and highways with steel bridges.

The Bates Ferry Trail offers a fascinating glimpse into the past, tracing the footsteps of travelers from the 18th, 19th, and 20th centuries. This trail once formed a vital link between the communities of Charleston and Camden. While crossing rivers is a relatively simple task today, it was a significant challenge in the 18th century. Bridges were difficult and expensive to construct, making ferries an essential means of transportation for people, wagons, livestock, and goods.

Just east of the trailhead, on Bates Old River (a former channel of the Congaree River), lies McCord's Ferry, one of the earliest historic crossings in the Midlands region. Bates Ferry itself began operations in the 1800s, ceased briefly at the turn of the century, and then resumed service between 1910 and 1923. It played a crucial role in maintaining this historic route and ensuring safe passage between communities.

In 1923, the Bates Ferry Bridge replaced the ferry service. Remnants of this bridge can still be seen at the end of the trail today. The Bates Ferry Bridge was subsequently replaced by US Highway 601 Bates Bridge in 1949, which was further replaced in 2012. By exploring the Bates Ferry Trail, visitors can gain a deeper appreciation for the region's rich history and the vital role that ferries played in its development.

Site 2: Trailhead

The Bear's-Foot Trail is a scenic and historic path that offers visitors a unique opportunity to experience nature's beauty. As you stroll along the wide, mowed path, you'll be following in the footsteps of those who came before. The trail's unimproved surface makes for easy walking, allowing you to enjoy the journey at your own pace.

One of the highlights of the trail is the abundance of Bear's-foot flowers, which bloom in vibrant yellow during the late spring and early fall. These tall, upright plants have large, irregularly-shaped leaves and clusters of small, yellow flowers. Bear's-foot is a popular nectar and pollen source for butterflies, attracting species like swallowtails and skippers. Additionally, this plant has long been recognized for its medicinal properties, used by both Native Americans and early settlers.

Beyond Bear's-foot, the trail is home to a variety of other plants, including wingstem, dayflower, butterfly pea, wild yam vine, germander, and blackberry. These plants add color and diversity to the landscape, creating a visually stunning experience.

The Bear's-Foot Trail isn't just for humans. Animals also use the path as a thoroughfare. Keep an eye out for signs of white-tailed deer, feral hogs, and wild turkeys. The small ponds along the trail are popular with wood ducks and river otters, while Great Blue Herons can sometimes be spotted fishing in the floodwaters.

Site 3: Side Trails

Bates Ferry Trail offers a variety of side trails that can provide additional exploration opportunities. While there's only one side trail branching off to the right, leading to the General Greene Tree, numerous side trails can be found on the left side of the main trail. Many of these side trails are dead ends, previously used for accessing hunting plots and stands maintained by the Kingville Hunt Club. If you're feeling adventurous, these side trails can offer similar features to the main trail, making them worth exploring.

Flooding and Trail Conditions

It's important to be aware of the potential for flooding on Bates Ferry Trail. Depending on the time of year, especially during the winter months, portions of the trail may be impassable due to high water levels. As you walk along the trail, you might encounter signs of flooding. Exercise caution when crossing flooded areas, as the water can be deeper and move faster than it appears. Always use your best judgment to determine if a section of the trail is safe to traverse.

Monitoring Water Levels

To help anticipate flooding on Bates Ferry Trail, you can monitor the Trezevant's Landing flood gage on the Upper Santee River. This information is available online and provides current and historical water levels. While the flood stage for the Congaree River is set at 80 feet, flooding on the trail becomes significant at 81 feet. When the water level reaches 82 feet or higher, the lower-lying portion of the trail at the specified location becomes impassable. By checking weather conditions and the Santee River flood gage, you can make informed decisions about your trail exploration.

Site 4: Side Trail to General Greene Tree

About 0.4 miles along the main trail, look for a side trail branching off to your right. If you pass a narrow pond covered in duckweed on your left, you've gone too far. This pond is actually one of the "borrow" pits used to excavate soil for the early 20th-century causeway you're walking on.

The side trail leads you across a steel deck bridge over Bates Old River, the former 1852 Congaree River channel. Before crossing, take a moment to admire the bridge's unique structure—it's actually a flat-bed trailer with the undercarriage and wheels still attached! From the bridge, you can survey the former river channel and spot a wide, curved lake (an ox-bow lake) that was cut off from the main river channel during the 1852 flood.

A Note of Caution: The portion of the trail beyond the bridge can flood easily. If the trail is covered in water, do not proceed. There are washed-out sections that can be dangerous when wet.

Site 5: General Greene Tree

As you venture deeper into the Congaree National Park, the trail will guide you towards a remarkable natural wonder. Once the path takes a leftward turn, you'll be greeted by the sight of the General Greene Tree. This majestic baldcypress stands tall, its massive trunk measuring an astonishing 30 feet in circumference. Its base, known as a "knee," rises to an impressive height of 8 feet and is nestled within a nearby slough.

The General Greene Tree holds a unique distinction within Congaree National Park. It boasts the largest circumference of any baldcypress discovered within the park's boundaries and is estimated to be several centuries old. This ancient tree has endured the test of time, its survival attributed to a fortuitous hollow center that rendered it unsuitable for logging during the region's timber-harvesting era.

As you gaze upon the General Greene Tree, take a moment to appreciate its historical significance. The tree is named in honor of Nathanael Greene, a prominent Revolutionary War general who met with Francis Marion at nearby McCord's Ferry following the Battle of Fort Motte.

Nearby, you'll find remnants of the park's logging past. Two massive baldcypress stumps serve as silent witnesses to the peak of cypress logging in the Congaree and upper Santee Watershed, which occurred around the turn of the 19th century. These stumps stand as a stark reminder of the park's transformation from a heavily exploited landscape to a protected wilderness.

After taking in the sights and stories surrounding the General Greene Tree and the historical stumps, retrace your steps along the main trail, continuing your exploration of the Congaree National Park's diverse ecosystems and rich history.

Site 7: Bates Ferry Landing

At the end of the Bates Ferry Trail, you'll find yourself on the northeast bank of the Congaree River. This stretch of the river was once dry land, but over time, the river carved a new channel, beginning in the early 1800s. By 1852, the river had completely abandoned its old course (now known as Bates Old River).

Bates Ferry: A River Crossing

This is where Bates Ferry once operated, providing a safe way for people to cross the river on the road connecting Camden and Charleston. The ferry was in service from the 1840s until the late 1800s and was later reopened in 1910 by J.M. Bates and other automotive enthusiasts.

The Bates Ferry Bridge

In 1923, a bridge was built at this site, thanks to the efforts of Mr. Bates. However, this bridge was short-lived. A major flood closed it for two years, and in the 1940s, just before the opening of the US Highway 601 bridge, a truck fell through its deteriorating deck.

Exploring the Riverbanks

When the water levels are low, you can explore the banks of the Congaree River. Be cautious, though, as the banks can be quite steep. Along the banks, you may find remnants of the old 1923 bridge and evidence of the road that once continued to Charleston on the opposite bank in Calhoun County.

Difficulty:

Easy

Type of Hike:

Out-and-back

Dogs on leash are allowed

It is suitable for families with kids

Length:

2.3 miles (round trip)

Estimated Time to Complete:

About 40 minutes

Accessibility:

The trail is generally accessible, with a paved surface.

Trailhead Elevation:

Approximately 40 feet

Total Elevation Gain:

Minimal

Highest Elevation:

Approximately 50 feet

Ability:

Suitable for most people, including those with moderate fitness levels.

Features:

- Scenic views of the Congaree River
- Hardwood forest with towering trees
- Opportunities for birdwatching and wildlife viewing

Allowed Uses:

Hiking

Trail Surface:

Paved

Best Time to Hike:

The trail is enjoyable year-round, but spring and fall offer pleasant temperatures and less humidity. Avoid peak summer months for a more comfortable experience.

Tips

Enjoy the Scenery: The Bates Ferry Trail offers stunning views of the Congaree River and surrounding floodplain forest. Take your time to appreciate the beauty of the natural world.

Look for Wildlife: Keep your eyes peeled for deer, alligators, and a variety of bird species. You may also encounter feral hogs.

Explore Side Trails: The Bates Ferry Trail has several side trails that lead to interesting features, such as the General Greene Tree, one of the largest bald cypress trees in the park.

Moderate Hikes

Weston Lake Trail

Trailhead: Harry Hampton Visitor Center

Description:

The Weston Lake Loop Trail offers a captivating exploration of Congaree National Park's ancient and diverse ecosystem. Starting at the terminus of the Sims Trail, this 2.0-mile loop leads visitors to the Elevated Boardwalk, providing stunning views of the surrounding wetlands. The entire round trip from the Harry Hampton Visitor Center is approximately 4.5 miles, offering ample opportunities to immerse oneself in the park's natural beauty.

As you traverse the Weston Lake Loop Trail, you'll encounter a variety of unique habitats, including Cedar Creek, Weston Lake Slough, and Weston Lake itself. These waterways play a vital role in the park's ecology, supporting a rich diversity of plant and animal life. The trail's proximity to these areas allows visitors to experience firsthand the intricate connections between the forest, wetlands, and waterways.

One of the highlights of the Weston Lake Loop Trail is the opportunity to witness the park's old-growth forest. This ancient woodland, dating back centuries, showcases the characteristics that inspired advocates in the 1950s and 1970s to preserve Congaree Swamp. The towering trees, dense undergrowth, and intricate network of vines create a truly awe-inspiring environment.

Congaree National Park is renowned for its exceptional biodiversity, thanks to the age of its forest, the constant process of ecological succession, and the replenishment of its soil through periodic flooding by the Congaree River. As a result, the park has been recognized as a Globally Important Bird Area, a Ramsar Wetlands of International Importance, and an International Biosphere Reserve.

Wildlife sightings are common on the Weston Lake Loop Trail. Keep your eyes peeled for deer, raccoons, rat snakes, and feral hogs. Listen for the calls of red-bellied woodpeckers, red-shouldered hawks, and pileated woodpeckers, which can be heard year-round. Along Cedar Creek, you may spot wood ducks, though their alarm calls are often heard before the birds themselves are seen. During the summer months, look for the vibrant colors of northern parula warblers and prothonotary warblers.

Legend

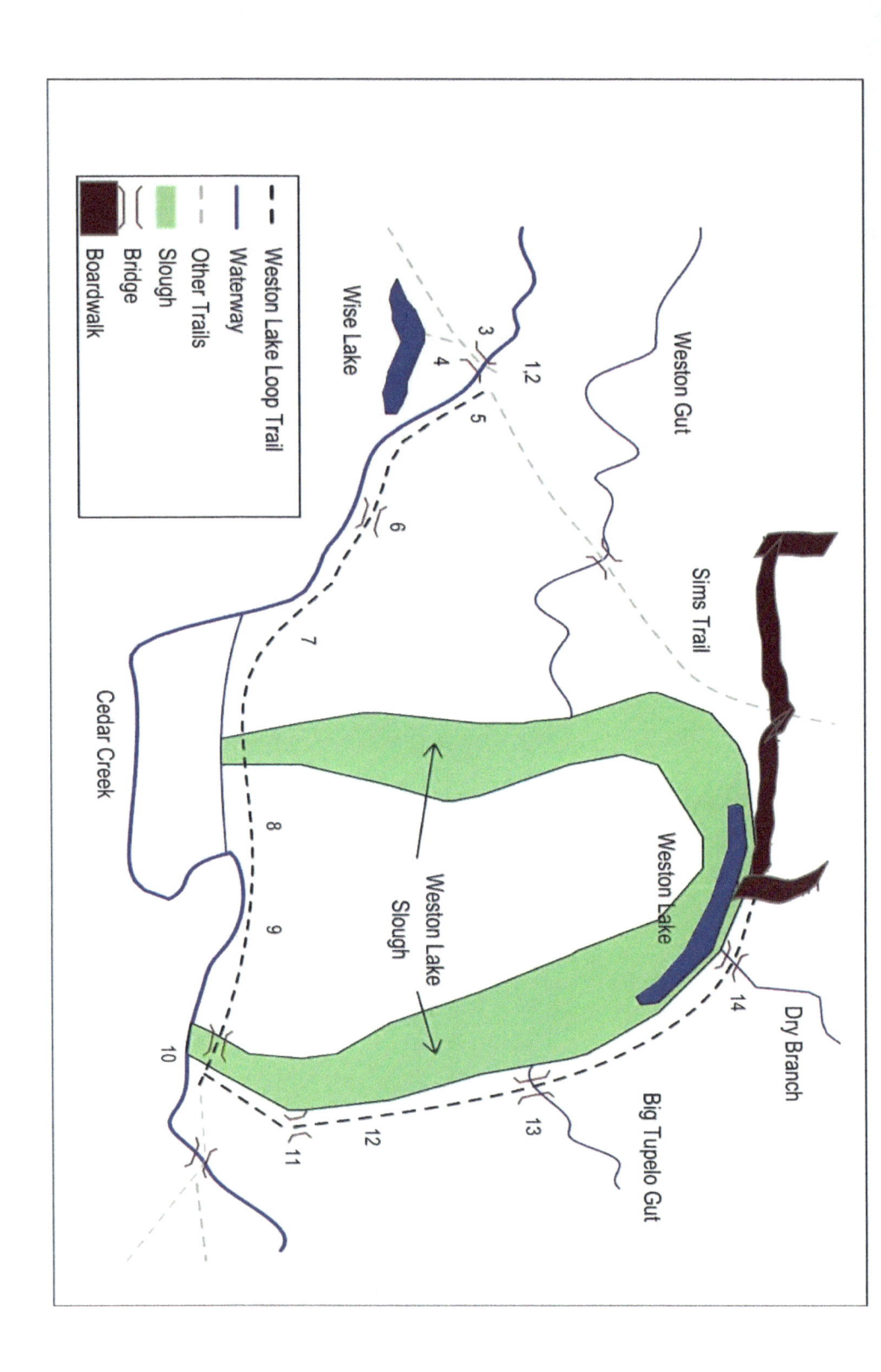

- — — Weston Lake Loop Trail
- ——— Waterway
- - - - Other Trails
-](Slough (green)
- ⬛ Bridge
- ▬ Boardwalk

Labels on map: Wise Lake, Weston Gut, Sims Trail, Cedar Creek, Weston Lake Slough, Weston Lake, Dry Branch, Big Tupelo Gut

Numbered points: 1,2 · 3 · 4 · 5 · 6 · 7 · 8 · 9 · 10 · 11 · 12 · 13 · 14

Site 1: Cedar Creek

At the trail junction, Cedar Creek is visible to your right and directly ahead. In the vicinity, you'll find several monitoring stations, including a stream gaging station equipped with a solar-powered satellite uplink, an inactive groundwater monitoring station, and an old well. The data collected by the stream gaging station is accessible through a link on the park's website, providing real-time information about flooding conditions within the park.

As a general guideline, when the water level at the gage reaches six feet, surface trails within the park may start to flood. At eight feet, portions of the Low Boardwalk may become submerged. If the water level rises to twelve feet, even parts of the Elevated Boardwalk could be inundated! It's important to remember that these are just rough estimates. For the most up-to-date information on flooding conditions, please visit the Visitor Center's Information Desk.

Site 2: Old Field

The trail junction where you stand marks the site of the former Cedar Creek Hunt Club cabin, a raised structure that once stood behind you. This cabin replaced an earlier one built by the United States Hunt Club, a name chosen to discourage poaching.

Open areas like this are scattered throughout the park, remnants of former feed plots for game, old logging decks, or agricultural fields. Through a process known as forest succession, these open spaces are gradually transforming into "old field" habitats. Fast-growing, sun-loving trees like sweetgum and loblolly pine compete with blackberries and grape vines for space. This old field is rapidly evolving into a dense forest, making it difficult to recognize as a former clearing.

While the forest closes in, take advantage of the remaining open sky to spot soaring birds. Look for Mississippi kites in summer or red-shouldered hawks year-round. A nearby swamp chestnut oak tree offers a unique feature: its unusually large acorns.

The Weston Lake Loop Trail turns left along Cedar Creek, but before you embark on that journey, you'll cross Cedar Creek bridge to visit Wise Lake.

Site 3: Cedar Creek Bridge B

As you journey through Congaree National Park, take a moment to pause at the Bannister Bridge. From this vantage point, you can observe the serene beauty of Cedar Creek as it gracefully meanders through the floodplain. Cedar Creek holds a special significance within the park, being the sole Outstanding National Resource Water in South Carolina. This designation underscores its exceptional natural and recreational value.

Paddling enthusiasts will find Cedar Creek an irresistible draw. The Cedar Creek Wilderness Trail offers two convenient launch points: Bannister Bridge and South Cedar Creek. Embark on a tranquil canoe or kayak adventure along this scenic waterway, immersing yourself in the natural beauty that surrounds you.

Site 4: Wise Lake Spur

Beyond the bridge, you'll find a sign marking the trailhead for Oakridge Trail and River Trail. Take note of the two dominant mid-sized tree species here: American holly and pawpaw. You may have noticed holly at the start of the Low Boardwalk — it thrives in a variety of habitats at the park. Pawpaw, with its large leaves, is one of the dominant understory trees in elevated areas of the park. Pawpaw fruit matures in late August and early September. The lobed green fruit speckled with black dots has edible creamy flesh inside encasing large, flat black seeds. The leaves turn a soft lemon yellow in the fall—a reliable source of fall color in the park.

Just beyond the trail sign, you'll come across Wise Lake, an oxbow lake. Over a thousand years ago, it was a river meander of the Congaree. Over time, the river cut a new, shorter channel, leaving the old meander behind. The Congaree River has continued to migrate to the south over the landscape and now lies about two miles away. Oxbow lakes eventually fill with sediment and become sloughs or ponds. A shallow oxbow like Wise Lake would typically be near the end of its lifecycle, but Wise Lake empties through a marshy outlet into Cedar Creek. This connection helps to scour sediments from Wise Lake, preventing it from filling in with silt.

Here, you'll see cypress knees like those you saw along the Sims Trail. One theory holds that cypress knees help the trees with gas exchange; the knees may also be anchors or counterweights that allow a cypress tree to grow large and still remain upright in wet soil.

Site 5: Leaving Old Field

Retrace your steps across the Cedar Creek Bridge and turn right to continue on Weston Lake Loop Trail. This section of the trail follows the north bank of Cedar Creek for 1.2 miles. As you re-enter the forest, you will see a substantial understory of pawpaw trees on your left. This portion of the trail introduces you to most of the dominant hardwood species found on the Congaree floodplain.

A large swamp chestnut oak tree stands to the left. If you keep your eye out for the light scaly bark, chestnut-like leaves and large acorns, you will notice several other large swamp chestnut oak trees on the trail. A few mid-sized sugarberry stand nearby. Look for the smooth gray bark (similar to American beech) often obscured by warty growths.

Farther on, you will find two examples of hardwood species to your right: a laurel oak and then a tall sweetgum. Laurel oaks are easy to spot in the winter; unlike other deciduous trees, they keep most of their leaves throughout the year. Sweetgum can be recognized by their star-shaped leaves and spiky gumballs. The park has an uncountable number of large sweet gum, including the former national champion tree.

Site 6: Boys Scout Bridge

The next destination is a small bridge marked "BSA Troop 199". As you approach the bridge, keep your eyes peeled for several interesting features along the trail.

To your left, you may have already noticed shallow rectangular depressions at a diagonal to the trail. These features, which look too regular to be natural depressions, are borrow pits. They were created when the trail was originally a jeep road for the hunt club.

On the right, look for a "walking" maple. This unusual tree is a result of a winged red maple seed that landed on a tupelo or cypress stump years ago. The maple extended its roots over and through the old stump, eventually causing the stump to rot away. This left only the maple trunk and its pedestal roots, creating the illusion of a walking tree.

Past the bridge, you will encounter another dominant tree species: a large, leaning cherrybark oak. This majestic tree is a striking feature of the landscape.

As you continue your journey, the trail hugs the bank of Cedar Creek. You will eventually pass by a large loblolly pine at the edge of the creek. This pine is somewhat isolated, but you will see numerous others later on. It's interesting to note that young loblollies are rarely seen in the park. This suggests that the conditions that favored their growth in the past no longer exist.

Site 7: Trail joins Slough Edge

After following the bank of Cedar Creek, the trail continues straight along a former channel of Cedar Creek. The creek itself briefly jogs to the south.

Site 8: Trail returns to the bank of Cedar Creek

Cedar Creek soon makes a northward turn, rejoining the trail. This is a picturesque spot where you can step off the trail to observe Cedar Creek at its confluence with both the trail and the slough. Take note of the significant damage to the base of several of the nearby trees, particularly the sweetgum. Beavers have stripped away the bark to access the sweet inner cambium layer.

This practice of removing bark can girdle the trees, potentially leading to their death. Such beaver activity is commonly seen along the trail. While beavers are a native species, their ponds provide benefits to a diverse range of species within this bottomland ecosystem.

Site 9: Small Bridge

The trail winds its way through a picturesque landscape, offering a glimpse into the natural beauty of the area. As you continue your journey, you'll come across a small bridge that spans a gentle stream.

Beyond the bridge, to your left, stands a majestic sycamore tree. Its unique appearance, with patterned bone-white bark, large leaves, and round seed capsules that burst into feathery seeds, makes it easy to spot. Sycamores are commonly found along elevated ground near river channels, and their presence in the floodplain interior can be a sign of a former river course.

Keep your eyes peeled as you explore the trail, as this area can be a prime spot for observing the fascinating six-spotted tiger beetle. This iridescent green beetle is named for the six inconspicuous white spots on the edge of its wing-cases. If you're lucky, you might catch a glimpse of this elusive creature darting across the path.

Site 10: Bridge C – Weston Lake Slough

After traversing 1.2 miles, the trail crosses Weston Lake Slough over a significant bridge (Bridge C). A slough is a large, elongated depression in the floodplain that remains wet for most of the year. These depressions often originate as oxbow lakes that have filled in with sediments carried by the river during floods. Sloughs are typically populated with wetland trees like tupelo and cypress, but may also harbor aquatic marsh plants such as sedges. Sedge, a grass-like native plant, is often an emergent vegetation, growing above the surface of shallow or seasonal wetlands. While sedge species can be challenging to distinguish, some varieties in the park have unique seedheads that aid identification.

Keep an eye out for signs of beaver activity in this area. Beavers have historically dammed Weston Lake Slough both upstream and downstream of the bridge, constructing a lodge upstream. Although the dams have mostly eroded, their remnants can still be seen. Beavers often utilize baldcypress and water tupelo as anchors for their dams. As you look upstream, you might notice a large baldcypress with a damaged top at the mouth of Weston Lake Slough. This tree is representative of many cypress that were too damaged to be harvested by timber companies at the turn of the century.

Beyond the bridge, take a moment to observe the trail sign marking the intersection of Kingsnake Trail, Oakridge Trail, and Weston Lake Loop Trail. The trail now turns left (north), departing from Cedar Creek and following the edge of Weston Lake Slough through a vibrant stand of switchcane towards

Weston Lake. Shortly after the turn, pause to admire the impressive cherrybark oak located to the right of the trail.

Site 11: First Bridge beyond Oakridge Trail Junction

Stop at the next bridge to take in the view of Weston Lake Slough to your left. This slough plays a vital role in the ecosystem as a nursery for juvenile fish. Research conducted by the South Carolina Department of Natural Resources from 1999 to 2002 revealed its significance in supporting the early development of young fish species.

During flood events, the Congaree River overflows its banks, leading to the dispersal of adult fish across the floodplain for breeding purposes. As the floodwaters gradually recede, sloughs like Weston Lake become isolated from the main river and creek channels. This isolation creates a safe haven for juvenile fish, amphibians, crayfish, and other aquatic species, allowing them to thrive in the absence of larger predators.

Site 12: Beyond first bridge and gut crossing

Continuing past the bridge, keep an eye out for a downed water oak on the left side of Weston Lake slough. Despite its name, water oaks are not commonly found in floodplains. They prefer upland environments. Notice the "tip-up," the exposed root system of the fallen tree. This is a common feature in floodplains due to the high groundwater table. The roots cannot survive in constantly saturated soil. Over time, tip-ups erode and rot, creating "pit and mound complexes" that can persist long after the tree has decayed.

As you return to higher ground, you'll start to see more large loblolly pines. This area was once part of a 19th-century property called Pine Bluff, owned by the Weston family. The presence of these mature pines suggests that the Weston family may have attempted to cultivate this part of the floodplain in the 1800s.

Site 13: Big Tupelo Gut-Bridge D

At approximately 2.1 miles into your journey, you'll encounter a significant landmark: Bridge D. This bridge spans Big Tupelo Gut, a natural waterway that winds through the area. Just a short distance from the bridge, on the bank of the gut, stands an extraordinary natural wonder: the national champion loblolly pine. Towering at nearly 170 feet, it holds the title of the tallest tree in South Carolina. While its foliage may obscure its height during the summer months, it's easily visible in the winter.

To the right of the champion pine, you might find a companion tree that, although nearly as impressive, may partially obstruct your view. Look for the pine with a prominent horizontal limb extending to the right—this is the champion. A footpath, created by frequent use, leads to the pine. While not an official park trail, this "social trail" is a popular route for visitors, especially those interested in fishing.

As you continue your journey past Bridge D, keep an eye out for a distinctive feature on your right: the dark, smooth, and spiraling supplejack vines. These vines have regularly spaced holes around their trunks. These holes are the work of yellow-bellied sapsuckers, a woodpecker species that spends its winters in the park. These birds chisel the holes to collect sap, which serves as a food source. Additionally, the holes can trap insects, providing a supplementary food source for sapsuckers and other wildlife.

Site 14: Dry Branch

Before continuing on your journey, take a moment to explore the scenic Dry Branch. This clear-flowing stream offers a refreshing contrast to the sloughs and guts you've encountered so far. While trees have recently obstructed its path, Dry Branch remains a year-round feature, eventually emptying into Weston Lake.

Joining the Weston Lake Loop Trail

As you venture onward, the Weston Lake Loop Trail will intersect with the elevated portion of the Boardwalk Loop Trail. To continue your exploration, rejoin the main trail and make a sharp right to reach the Weston Lake overlook and the Elevated Boardwalk. This detour will add approximately 1.4 miles to your journey before returning to the Visitor Center.

Returning to the Visitor Center

If you prefer a more direct route back to the Visitor Center, turn left onto the Low Boardwalk. This option will take you approximately 1.2 miles to your destination.

Difficulty: Easy to moderate

Type of Hike: Loop

Dogs on leash are allowed

The trail is suitable for families

Length: Approximately 4.5 miles

Estimated Time to Complete: 2-3 hours

Accessibility: The trail is generally accessible, but there are some areas with uneven terrain.

Trailhead Elevation: 55 feet

Total Elevation Gain: Minimal

Highest Elevation: 65 feet

Ability: Suitable for most fitness levels.

Features: Scenic views of Weston Lake, Cedar Creek, and old-growth forest. Great for birdwatching and wildlife observation.

Allowed Uses: Hiking, cycling

Trail Surface: Mostly packed dirt and gravel.

Best Time to Hike: Spring and fall are ideal, with mild temperatures and fewer crowds. Avoid summer for hot and humid conditions.

Fork Swamp Trail

Trailhead: Located off US 601, a significant distance from the main park entrance and visitor center.

Description:

Fork Swamp Trail is the ninth formal trail in Congaree National Park. This 0.6-mile loop trail follows the banks of Bates Old River, a former channel of the Congaree River, offering excellent opportunities for water recreation and birdwatching. The trail is conveniently located along the US 601 corridor, a prime area for future park development. It's also relatively close to the Bates Ferry Trail and the park's newest land acquisition. The park plans to extend Fork Swamp Trail and create a larger outer loop that will connect to the junction of Bates Old River and the Congaree River.

This short trail offers several unique attractions. Fork Swamp Trail provides easy access to an informal paddling launch on Bates Old River, a popular spot for observing River Otters during the late fall and early winter. The trail's proximity to the

Congaree River allows visitors to enjoy stunning views of soaring birds, including Bald Eagles and Ospreys. Former hunt club clearings and a wet meadow offer diverse habitats that attract a variety of birds and other wildlife.

Safety First: Please note that the eastern (downstream) end of the park is prone to more frequent and prolonged flooding compared to the main trail system to the west. Never hike on flooded trails alone, and always exercise caution when encountering unexpected bodies of water. Moving water can be extremely dangerous, regardless of depth. Take necessary precautions and avoid risks whenever possible.

Fork Swamp Trail Map

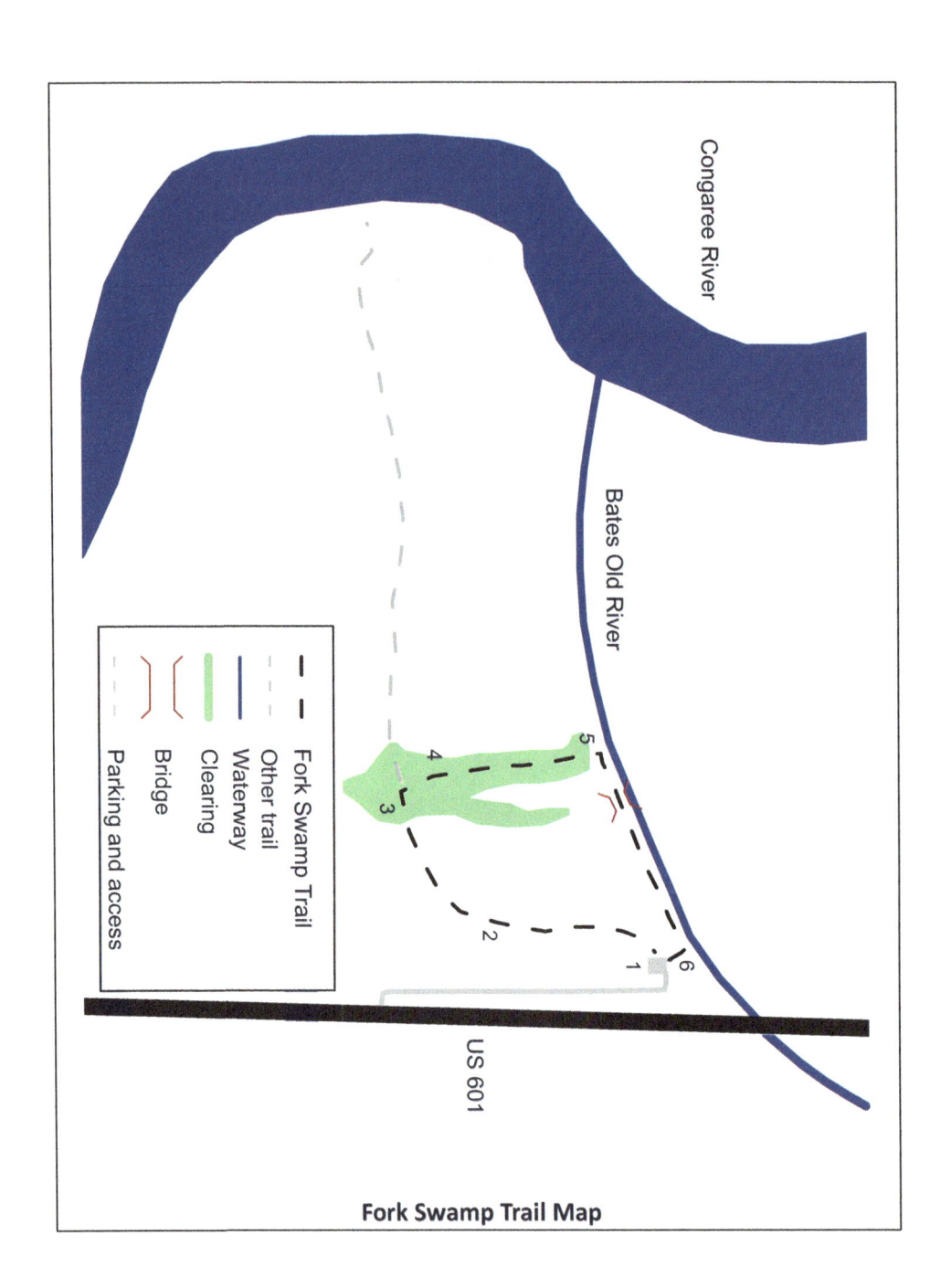

74

Site 1: Trailhead and Kiosk

At the end of the parking lot, you'll find a trailhead marked by an interpretive kiosk. From here, two paths diverge: one continues straight ahead, while the other turns to the right. Both paths will eventually loop back to the parking lot, forming a circular route. Before embarking on your journey, take a moment to read the informative panels at the kiosk. These panels offer valuable insights into the history, geology, and potential hazards of Bates Old River.

Learn about the fascinating formation of Bates Old River, a former channel of the Congaree River. Discover the unique features of the floodplain, including Sampson Island, a wind-formed dune that has been used by humans for millennia. Additionally, the panels provide information about the historical significance of the riverbank as a travel route dating back to the mid-1700s.

Site 2: Trees with multiple trunks

Begin your journey at the park kiosk. Head straight ahead on the designated trail, keeping a sharp eye out for trail markers. Specifically, look for markers with the number "9" clearly displayed. This indicates that you're on the Fork Swamp Trail, the 9th trail in the park. Paying attention to these markers is crucial to stay on the correct path, especially during hazardous conditions like flooding.

Prepare for Varied Trail Conditions

The Fork Swamp Trail can be somewhat overgrown with grass and sedge. To accommodate visitors, the park periodically clears a path from the parking lot to the banks of Bates Old River. However, it's important to be prepared for varying trail conditions throughout your hike.

A History of Logging

As you walk along the trail, you'll notice that many of the trees have multiple trunks stemming from the same root system. These are known as re-sprouted trees, a sign that they were once cut down and have regrown from the stump. The abundance of re-sprouted trees in this area suggests that it was once a significant logging site. Although the trees have recovered and grown tall, the presence of these re-sprouted specimens indicates that this part of the park has a history of logging activity.

A Birder's Paradise

Fork Swamp Trail is an excellent spot for birdwatching. Keep your ears open for the distinctive song of the American Redstart, a colorful black songbird with orange patches on its wings and tail. This species typically breeds farther north but can be found nesting along the banks of South Carolina's coastal plain rivers, including the Congaree River.

Beware of Feral Hogs

While exploring the trail, you may encounter signs of feral hog activity, such as rooting and overturned soil. These animals can cause significant damage to the park's ecosystem by disrupting native plants and disturbing wildlife. Be cautious and avoid approaching feral hogs.

Site 3: Meadow

Farther along the trail, the dense forest gives way to a more open landscape. The treeline thins, revealing a large clearing dominated by tall brush and wetland plants like Black Willow and Crimson-eyed Rose Mallow. This creates a corridor for visitors to explore, although the area is prone to flooding. Be prepared to navigate around flooded meadows to continue your journey.

At the heart of the clearing, the trail splits into two directions. One path continues on the loop trail, while the other heads straight ahead. The forward path is currently unfinished and hasn't been officially designated. Congaree National Park plans to expand the Fork Swamp Trail in the near future, with this junction serving as the starting point for the outer loop. The outer loop will take visitors to the banks of the Congaree River and then follow Bates Old River back to the existing trail.

While exploring the meadow, take a moment to look up. This area is close to the confluence of the Congaree and Wateree Rivers, as well as the headwaters of Upper Santee Swamp. This makes it a prime habitat for a variety of bird species. In addition to common sightings like swallows and swifts, you may spot raptors such as Mississippi Kites, Bald Eagles, and Ospreys, or wading birds like Great Blue Herons, Great Egrets, and White Ibises.

Site 4: Metting of the trail and Bates Old River

In a short distance, you'll reach the banks of Bates Old River, a former river channel that's now often called "Dead River." Be cautious as you walk along the edge, especially if the water levels are high. The drop-off can be steep and the bank slippery.

Bates Old River was once the main channel of the Congaree River until a major flood in 1852 forced the river to change course. The section west of US 601 is narrower, while the part east of US 601 has become a popular fishing spot.

Riverbank Flora

As you walk along Bates Old River, you'll notice trees that are typically found in riverbank forests. One of the most common trees is the American Sycamore, with its distinctive mottled bark.

If you're hiking in the spring, you might encounter butterweed, a vibrant wildflower that can carpet the forest floor in certain years. While the floodplain isn't known for its wildflowers, Bates Old River offers a unique opportunity to witness this natural beauty.

Site 5: Water Recreation Informal put-In

The final stretch of the Fork Swamp Trail offers a serene and rewarding experience for nature enthusiasts. As you approach the parking lot, you'll find yourself in a prime spot for observing river otters. These playful creatures often utilize fallen tree trunks in the river as resting and dining areas, making it a great opportunity to catch a glimpse of their aquatic antics.

A Baldcypress Beauty

A standout feature of this area is a majestic Baldcypress tree, its towering presence dominating the Bates Old River's bank at low water levels. This ancient tree, a symbol of the South's wetlands, adds a touch of natural grandeur to the landscape.

A Convenient Access Point

For kayakers and canoeists, the trailhead provides an easy launch point onto the river. The gentle slope of the bank and proximity to the road make it a natural ramp, allowing for convenient access to the water. In the future, the park may consider adding some infrastructure to further enhance this entry point while minimizing environmental impact.

Exploring the Waterways

From the launch point, paddlers can embark on a scenic journey along Bates Old River and the Congaree River. Heading left for 0.7 miles, you'll reach the Congaree River, where you can paddle for 1.4 miles to SCDNR's Bates boat landing. A shuttle service can then transport you back to the Fork Swamp trailhead. Alternatively, paddling to the right under US 601 will lead you to the open portion of Bates Old River east of the highway. However, this section is more easily accessible from an unimproved landing located further north along US 601. Before setting off on your paddling adventure, be sure to consult the Congaree River Blue Trail map for important safety guidelines.

Returning to the Trailhead

After your exploration, the Fork Swamp Trail takes a sharp right turn, leading you directly back to the parking lot and interpretive signs. This marks the conclusion of your journey through this beautiful natural area.

Difficulty: Easy

Type of Hike: Loop

Dogs are allowed but on leash

Its is suitable for families

Length: 0.6 miles

Estimated Time to Complete: Approximately 30 minutes

Accessibility: The trail surface is mostly flat, making it accessible for most people.

Trailhead Elevation: Varies slightly, but generally low.

Total Elevation Gain: Minimal.

Highest Elevation: Low.

Ability: Suitable for most fitness levels, including beginners.

Features: Scenic views of Bates Old River, potential for wildlife sightings (e.g., birds, turtles).

Allowed Uses: Hiking, running

Trail Surface: Mostly flat and well-maintained.

Best Time to Hike: Year-round, but avoid peak summer months for cooler temperatures.

Tips

- **Follow the Markers:** The trail is marked with brown blazes. Pay attention to these markers to stay on the correct path, especially in areas with dense vegetation.
- **Enjoy the Scenery:** Take time to admire the towering trees, vibrant wildlife, and peaceful atmosphere.
- **Combine with Other Trails:** Fork Swamp Trail can be combined with other trails in the park, such as the Fireflies Trail or the Boardwalk Loop, for a longer adventure.
- **Consider a Guided Tour:** If you're new to the park or want to learn more about the area's history and ecology, consider joining a guided tour.
- **Visit During Peak Firefly Season:** If you're lucky enough to visit during late spring or early summer, you may witness a stunning display of fireflies lighting up the swamp.

Difficult Hikes

Oakridge Trail

Description:

Begin your hike at the Visitor Center breezeway and follow the Boardwalk Loop Trail south for a short distance. At the trail junction, turn left (east) onto the Boardwalk Loop Trail and continue until you reach Sims Trail. Turn right (south) onto Sims Trail and follow it for approximately 1.1 miles until you reach a junction with Weston Lake Loop Trail and Oakridge Trail near Cedar Creek.

Exploring the Old-Growth Forest

Congaree National Park is renowned for its ancient and towering old-growth bottomland forest, one of the largest and tallest hardwood forests in the southeastern United States. This hike offers a fantastic opportunity to experience the grandeur of these magnificent trees. Along the Boardwalk Loop and Weston Lake portions, you'll encounter bald cypress trees with their distinctive "knees" and water tupelo trees. As you venture deeper into the forest on the Oakridge Trail, you'll be surrounded by massive hardwoods, including ancient oaks and towering loblolly pines. Some of these colossal trees have earned the nickname "Redwoods of the East," and Congaree National Park is often referred to as the "Forest of Champions" due to its numerous state and national champion trees.

Navigating the Oakridge Trail

While the Oakridge Trail provides a captivating journey through the heart of the old-growth forest, it's important to be mindful of potential challenges. Fallen trees can occasionally obstruct the trail, requiring hikers to climb over or around them. Additionally, portions of the Oakridge Trail may flood more frequently than other trails, making it difficult to follow the path. To ensure a comfortable and enjoyable hike, consider wearing waterproof shoes.

Wildlife Encounters

Congaree National Park's floodplain location and long history of preservation have contributed to a diverse array of wildlife. Keep your eyes peeled for otters, deer, raccoons, snakes, and wild hogs. Birdwatchers may also encounter various species, including woodpeckers, red-shouldered hawks, warblers, wood ducks, and barred owls.

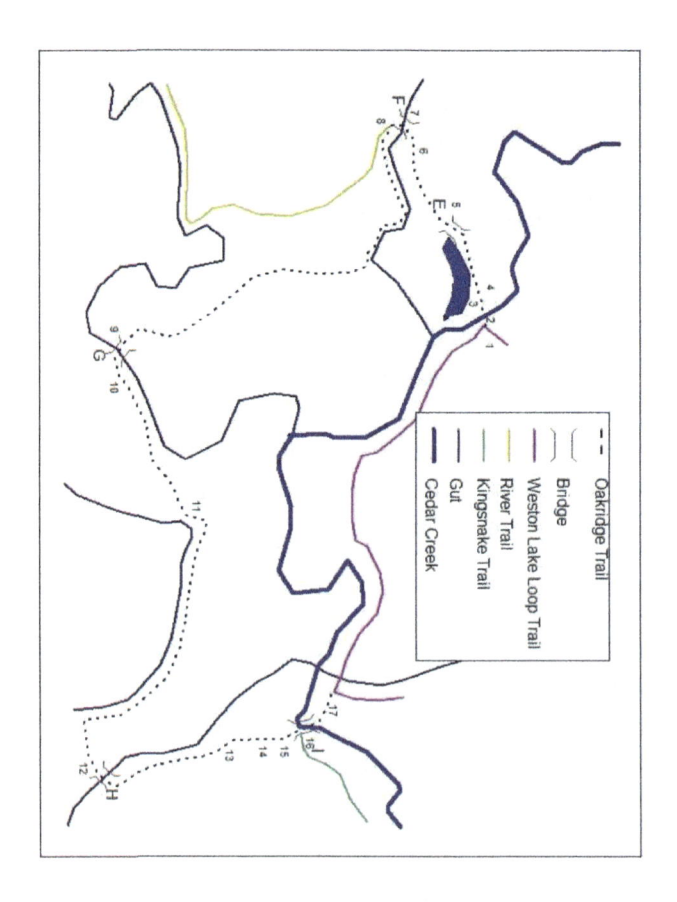

Site 1: Cedar Creek Water Trail

As you arrive at the Oakridge Trailhead, you'll be greeted by the peaceful sight of Cedar Creek flowing gently to your right. Near the creek, you'll notice several gauges that were once used to measure the water level. These gauges, supported by the park and the Friends of Congaree Swamp, have now been relocated to Bridge B (Site 2).

To give you an idea of the park's accessibility, keep in mind that when the water level at the Cedar Creek gauge reaches six feet, surface trails may be wet or even submerged. At eight feet, parts of the low boardwalk are likely underwater, while twelve feet may cause portions of the elevated boardwalk to be affected. However, it's important to note that these are general guidelines, and the most up-to-date information is always available at the Visitor Center.

If you're looking for a more adventurous experience, Cedar Creek offers a scenic water trail that can be explored by canoe or kayak. The trail, approximately 15 miles long, starts at Bannister Bridge and ends at the Congaree River. While the journey is generally enjoyable, be aware that natural debris in the creek can sometimes make navigation challenging. As you paddle along, you'll notice mile markers that help guide your way. This particular section of Cedar Creek is at mile 3.0, and you should encounter signs every half mile. Before embarking on your aquatic adventure, it's essential to check the current water level of Cedar Creek to ensure safe and enjoyable paddling.

Site 2: Cedar Creek Bridge

As you venture deeper into the park, you'll encounter Cedar Creek, a picturesque waterway that winds its way through the landscape. To safely traverse this scenic feature, you'll utilize Bridge B. Each bridge within the park is uniquely identified by a letter carved into a crossboard on its deck, making it easy to locate and navigate the trails.

A Pristine Body of Water

Cedar Creek holds a special significance. It has been designated as Outstanding Natural Resource Waters, a prestigious title bestowed upon bodies of freshwater that exhibit exceptional quality and have remained largely untouched by human intervention. This designation underscores the importance of preserving Cedar Creek's pristine condition and highlights the commitment to protecting its natural beauty for generations to come.

Site 3: Wise Lake Spur

Immediately after crossing Bridge B, you will see a sign marking the trailhead for the Oakridge Trail and the River Trail. To proceed onto the Oakridge Trail, make a slight right.

If you stay straight, about 50 yards ahead is Wise Lake, a small body of water ringed by bald cypress and water tupelo trees.

Site 4: Onto Oakridge Trail

The Oakridge Trail offers a captivating journey through the heart of the park. This 3.1-mile stretch, starting from the Visitor Center, eventually merges with the Weston Lake Loop Trail near Bridge C. Along the way, you'll encounter a diverse array of trees, each with its unique characteristics.

Water Tupelo and Bald Cypress: The Pillars of the Park

Two of the most iconic trees in the park are the water tupelo and the bald cypress. These aquatic trees thrive in the wet conditions of the floodplain. Both have flared trunks and "knees" that help them stay stable in water-saturated soil. The bald cypress is known for its deciduous needles, which it sheds in the fall, earning it the name "bald." In contrast, the water tupelo retains its leaves year-round. These trees are not only visually striking but also play a crucial role in the ecosystem, providing habitat and food for wildlife.

American Holly: A Year-Round Gem

As you continue along the Oakridge Trail, you'll be greeted by the evergreen American holly. This sub-canopy tree stands out with its bright red berries, which persist through the winter. While the berries may be bitter to humans, they are a valuable food source for various wildlife species.

Pawpaw: A Sweet Treat

Another notable tree you'll encounter on this trail is the pawpaw. This small tree produces large leaves and green fruit that ripens in late summer or early September. Native Americans and wildlife alike have enjoyed the sweet taste of pawpaw fruit for centuries.

As you explore the Oakridge Trail, take the time to appreciate the beauty and diversity of the trees that call this park home. From the towering bald cypress to the vibrant American holly, each species has a unique story to tell.

Site 5: Bridge E- End of Wise Lake

At the outset of the Oakridge Trail, you'll be greeted by the tranquil Wise Lake and its adjacent slough on your left. A slough is a low-lying area in a floodplain that retains water for extended periods. These sloughs are often teeming with bald cypress and water tupelo trees, adding to the serene ambiance. As you stroll past Wise Lake, keep an eye out for the impressive bald cypress trees that dot the landscape.

Switchcane and Canebrakes

As you continue along the trail beyond Bridge E, you'll encounter a plant that resembles miniature bamboo—this is switchcane, a native species to South Carolina. It typically doesn't grow taller than two meters and forms dense stands known as canebrakes. These canebrakes provide vital shelter for wildlife.

Majestic Oaks

The Oakridge Trail is renowned for its towering trees, especially oaks. Two prominent species that thrive here are the cherrybark oak and the swamp chestnut oak. The cherrybark oak is a rapidly growing tree that can reach heights of 100 to 130 feet. Its leaves are distinctive with 5 to 11 pointed lobes. The swamp chestnut oak, as the name suggests, has leaves similar to chestnut leaves. It typically grows to heights of 50 to 80 feet.

Identifying the Oaks

To help you distinguish between these two oak species on your hike, observe their leaves. The cherrybark oak has larger leaves with more pointed lobes, while the swamp chestnut oak has smaller, more rounded leaves. Keep your eyes peeled for these magnificent trees as you explore the Oakridge Trail.

Site 7: Bridge F Hammond Gut

As you venture deeper into the Congaree National Park, you'll soon encounter Bridge F, spanning Hammond Gut. This small stream is one of several "guts" found within the park. Unlike creeks, guts are typically shallower and shorter, often drying up or nearly so during dry spells. However, they play a vital role in the floodplain ecosystem. When heavy rains cause flooding, guts act as natural channels, helping to disperse water throughout the floodplain. As floodwaters recede, they flow back into the main creek and river channels, ensuring a healthy balance.

The Harry Hampton Bald Cypress

Hammond Gut serves as a significant landmark for park rangers and visitors familiar with the area. It's a key point for locating the Harry Hampton Bald Cypress, a towering testament to the park's ancient heritage.

Harry Hampton's Legacy

Over six decades ago, Harry Hampton, a writer and editor for The State newspaper, initiated a one-man crusade to protect the Congaree River Floodplain. Despite facing initial opposition, his vision of preserving the Congaree Swamp eventually gained traction. Thanks to his tireless efforts, the park was established, and his contributions were honored by naming the Visitor Center and a magnificent bald cypress tree after him.

The Harry Hampton Tree

The Harry Hampton Tree stands as a centerpiece within a grove of other ancient cypress trees. This towering giant boasts a height of 133 feet and a circumference of 23 feet 9 inches. It's the largest bald cypress in the area, a testament to the park's enduring beauty and ecological significance.

The park and the Friends of the Congaree Swamp regularly offer guided tours of notable trees, including the Harry Hampton Tree.

Site 8: River Trail Trailhead

Shortly after you cross Bridge F, you will come to the trailhead for the River Trail. The entire River Trail hike (including the Boardwalk Loop, Weston Lake Loop and Oakridge portions) is approximately 10 miles long. The River Trail provides access to the Congaree River.

Site 9: Bridge G – Boggy Gut

You will soon cross Boggy Gut using Bridge G. Boggy Gut is another one of the primary guts that winds through the park. As you cross over Bridge G and continue on the trail, Boggy Gut will be on your left.

Site 10: Boggy Gut; Ole Man Rogan

Boggy Gut, a place steeped in African American history and folklore, is said to be the home of the restless spirit of Ole Man Rogan. This cruel slave trader, known for his ruthless separation of slave families, once lived in the area. According to local folklore, after his death, Ole Man Rogan was denied entry into heaven and condemned to wander Boggy Gut forever as punishment for his cruelty. This story reflects a common theme in African American folklore: the eternal punishment of those who mistreated African Americans.

As you explore Boggy Gut, keep an eye out for beaver-damaged trees. Beavers are known to peel away the bark at the base of trees, particularly sweetgum trees, to eat the inner layer. This practice can weaken and even kill the tree. Look for recent damage by the sweet, pungent scent emitted by the injured tree.

Site 11: Deep Jackson Gut

About halfway between Bridge G and Bridge H, you'll encounter Deep Jackson Gut on your right. This narrow waterway parallels the Oakridge Trail until it merges with Frenchman's Pond, a picturesque slough visible from the trail. Deep Jackson Gut serves as a connection between Frenchman's Pond and the Congaree River.

During periods of high-water levels in the Congaree River, floodwaters can overflow into the floodplain, following channels like Deep Jackson Gut. This gut often experiences flooding before other surface trails, earning its name. If you find this section of the trail submerged, be prepared to retrace your steps. Rising waters can obscure the trail's path or conceal the presence of the gut.

Site 12: Bridge H-Running Gut

As you venture deeper into Congaree National Park, you'll soon encounter Running Gut, a significant waterway that plays a vital role in the park's ecosystem. This natural channel helps drain excess water from the floodplain, ultimately carrying it towards the Congaree River. While some smaller guts might dry up seasonally, Running Gut is a perennial stream, flowing consistently throughout the year.

Your path will take you across Bridge H, providing a convenient passage over this important waterway. Continuing your journey, approximately 0.1 miles beyond Bridge H, keep your eyes peeled to the left. There, you'll be greeted by a truly impressive sight: a massive cherrybark oak. This towering tree, with its characteristic furrowed bark and spreading branches, stands as a testament to the park's ancient and resilient forest.

Site 14: Large Loblolly Pines

As you continue your journey along the Oakridge Trail, you'll begin to notice something unusual: tall, slender trees with long, needle-like leaves. These are loblolly pine trees, a species that is abundant in South Carolina. While pine trees are commonly found in many parts of the state, they are not typically seen in hardwood floodplains.

However, in this particular area, loblolly pines have managed to thrive. The rich, moist soil here provides the ideal conditions for their growth, allowing them to flourish and reach impressive heights. In fact, just a short distance away on the Weston Lake Loop Trail, you'll encounter the largest loblolly pine in all of America. Standing at nearly 170 feet tall, it's a testament to the unique characteristics of this forest.

Despite the presence of these towering pines, it's unusual to see young loblolly trees in this area. This suggests that the conditions that once favored their growth may no longer exist. Perhaps changes in the local environment, such as alterations to the floodplain or competition from other plant species, have limited their ability to regenerate.

Site 15: Kingsnake Trail Junction

The Kingsnake Trail is a popular hiking trail in the area. It is located right before Bridge I, and the trailhead is 5.8 miles from the Visitor Center. The trail is 11.7 miles long and includes the Boardwalk Loop, Weston Lake Loop, and Oakridge portions. It is important to note that the Kingsnake Trail is not a loop trail, as indicated on the trailhead sign.

Site 17: Rejoining Weston Loop Trail

Shortly after crossing Bridge, I, you'll veer right at the trail sign to rejoin the Weston Lake Loop Trail. Here, a striking sight awaits: a vast expanse of bald cypress trees partially submerged in water. This is Weston Lake Slough, a serene inlet that connects to Weston Lake further along the trail.

Elevated Boardwalk and Return

As you continue your journey, the Weston Lake Loop Trail will pass beneath the elevated section of the Boardwalk Loop Trail. After going under the boardwalk, turn left onto the lower boardwalk and follow it back to the Visitor Center. With Weston Lake on your left, simply follow the low boardwalk for approximately 1.2 miles to reach your starting point.

Difficulty:

The Oakridge Trail is considered an easy trail. It is suitable for hikers of all ages and abilities.

Type of hike:

The Oakridge Trail is a loop trail.

Dogs are allowed on the Oakridge Trail, but they must be kept on a leash at all times

Kids are allowed on the Oakridge Trail

Length:

The Oakridge Trail is 6.6 miles long.

Estimated time to complete:

The Oakridge Trail takes about 30 minutes to complete.

Accessibility:

The Oakridge Trail is accessible to people with disabilities. There is a boardwalk section of the trail that is wheelchair accessible.

Trailhead Elevation:

The Oakridge Trail starts at an elevation of 120 feet.

Total Elevation Gain:

The Oakridge Trail has a total elevation gain of 20 feet.

Highest Elevation:

The highest elevation on the Oakridge Trail is 140 feet.

Ability:

The Oakridge Trail is a great trail for beginners and families. It is also a good option for people who are looking for a short and easy hike.

Features:

The Oakridge Trail features a variety of features, including:

- A large sandbar
- A variety of trees, including huge uprooted trees, enormous deciduous and pine trees
- A variety of wildlife, including deer, wild hogs, alligators, and snakes

Allowed uses:

The Oakridge Trail is allowed for hiking and running only. Biking is not allowed on the trail.

Trail surface:

The Oakridge Trail is mostly dirt, with some sections of boardwalk.

Best time to hike:

The Oakridge Trail can be hiked year-round, but the best time to hike is in the spring and fall when the weather is mild.

River Trail

Trailhead: Located at the Harry Hampton Visitor Center.

Description:

The River Trail, a 10.4-mile loop adventure, offers visitors to Congaree National Park's western end a chance to delve into the heart of the park's ecosystem – the Congaree River. This trail is a favorite among backpackers and groups seeking an overnight adventure. Their destination? A breathtaking sandbar, the undisputed highlight of the hike.

Beyond the River and the Sandbar

The River Trail offers much more than just a scenic riverbank. As you hike, you'll be surrounded by towering old-growth hardwoods, a testament to the tireless preservation efforts of the 1950s, 60s, and 70s. Keep an eye out for the park's grand champion – a majestic cherrybark oak reaching an impressive 25 feet in circumference and towering 125 feet high.

The trail unfolds through various unique habitats. You'll traverse the park's distinctive river levee forest, a haven for a diverse range of wildlife rarely found elsewhere in the park. This includes breeding grounds for the American Redstart and the elusive Swainson's Warbler.

A stop at the sandbar provides a front-row seat to observe the river's residents. Watch out for Belted Kingfishers, Ospreys, and even Bald Eagles soaring overhead.

Finding the River Trail

Reaching the River Trail requires navigating a combination of three other trails. Start your journey at the Visitor Center breezeway and follow the Boardwalk Loop Trail south for 0.7 miles. Just past a small bridge, the Boardwalk Loop veers left, but you'll want to continue straight ahead onto the Weston Lake Loop Trail, marked with the number "3."

Follow the Weston Lake Loop for about 0.5 miles until you reach a junction with the Oakridge Trail (marked "4"). Here, you'll be 1.2 miles from the Visitor Center. Take the Oakridge Trail for another 0.5 miles until you reach Bridge F over Hammond Gut. Just past the bridge, you'll find the River Trail junction – turn right and follow signs marked with the number "5."

Important Note: This guide describes the 6.3-mile section of the River Trail that loops back to this junction. While the sites mentioned in this guide are numbered, there won't be any physical markers on the trail itself. Due to the park's designation as a national wilderness area, human interventions like signs are minimal. Most numbered locations correspond to natural features or historical markers, so their position should be fairly clear.

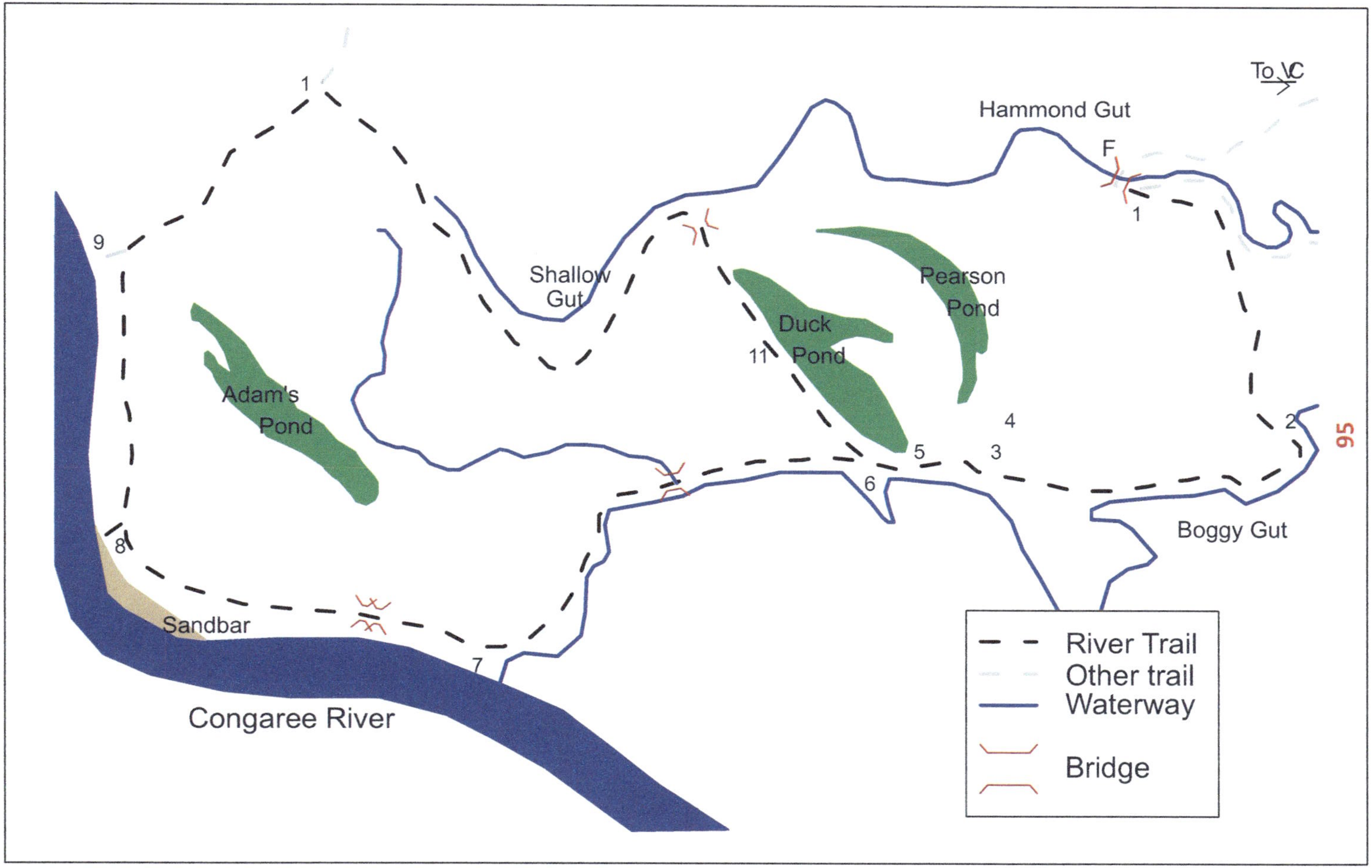
To VC
Hammond Gut
F
1
9
Shallow Gut
Pearson Pond
Duck Pond
11
Adam's Pond
4
2
5
3
6
Boggy Gut
8
Sandbar
7
Congaree River
River Trail
Other trail
Waterway
Bridge

Site 1: Oakridge Trail Junction

The River Trail, a scenic path that winds along the bank of Hammond Gut, offers a unique opportunity to explore the natural beauty of the area. Hammond Gut, a local term for a small, shallow stream, is a distinctive feature of the floodplain. These guts play a crucial role in flood control, channeling water from the Congaree River and helping to prevent flooding.

As you stroll along the River Trail, you'll be greeted by a vibrant tapestry of plants. In the spring and early summer, the trail is often adorned with Spotted Jewelweed, a captivating plant known for its orange blossoms and touch-sensitive seeds. The crushed leaves and stems of Spotted Jewelweed are believed to have medicinal properties, providing relief from poison ivy.

However, the trail is also home to an invasive species, Stiltgrass. This fast-spreading annual plant can form dense carpets on the forest floor, posing a challenge to native vegetation. The Southeast Coast Exotic Plant Management Team is working tirelessly to control the spread of invasive species, but Stiltgrass's rapid growth makes it a formidable adversary.

Site 2: Boggy Gut and Ole Man Rogan

Your hike will take you along Boggy Gut, a natural feature that offers scenic beauty and a touch of local lore. As you follow the trail, be sure to detour to the gut whenever possible. You might be lucky enough to spot a Great Blue Heron, Yellow-crowned Night Heron, or Barred Owl. These birds often frequent the gut, hunting for crayfish and salamanders.

Beyond its natural beauty, Boggy Gut is steeped in local history and folklore. It is said to be the home of the spirit of Ole Man Rogan, a cruel slave trader who once lived in the area. According to legend, Ole Man Rogan took pleasure in separating slave families, selling family members to different owners. He also loved fishing on Boggy Gut.

After his death, it is believed that Ole Man Rogan's restless spirit was condemned to wander Boggy Gut forever as a punishment for his cruelty. The rattle of chains, the cries of separated children, and Ole Man Rogan's cruel laughter are said to be heard along the gut. This story is a reflection of a common theme in African-American folklore: the eternal punishment for those who were cruel in life.

For more tales of Congaree, including the story of Ole Man Rogan, you can consult the two-volume set compiled by E.C.L. (Ned) Adams. This collection of folklore features stories gathered from local residents, including Thaddeus Goodson.

Site 3: Large Cherry bark Oak

As you journey along the trail, you'll encounter a truly impressive sight: the Cherrybark Oak. This towering hardwood, one of the largest in the park, boasts a circumference of over 23 feet. Its graceful branching pattern is a hallmark of its species, making it a standout among the forest canopy. The Cherrybark Oak is highly valued for its timber, which has been used in the furniture trade for veneer.

The Everlasting Baldcypress

Continuing your exploration, keep an eye out for an unusual multi-trunked Baldcypress on your left, near the edge of Boggy Gut. Baldcypress is renowned for its slow decay, earning it the nickname "the wood eternal." Historically, this species was highly prized for its shingles, which were used in roofing and siding. Unfortunately, the logging boom of the late 19th and early 20th centuries decimated many baldcypress populations in the southeastern United States. The old-growth baldcypress trees found in Congaree National Park are now rare and precious remnants of a bygone era.

Site 6: Trail Junction

As you reach the trail junction, the journey will take a left turn, following a clockwise loop that extends for approximately 3.7 miles. This loop will bring you back to the starting point, allowing you to fully explore the scenic beauty of the area.

Along this path, you'll be captivated by the majestic presence of several towering hardwoods. Keep an eye out for a pair of impressive beech trees, alongside additional cherrybark and a magnificent Shumard Oak. This initial segment of the River Trail offers a remarkable glimpse into the park's preserved old-growth bottomland hardwood forest, showcasing the natural beauty and diversity of the region.

Site 7: Congaree River and River Levee Forest

As you venture deeper into the forest, the first glimpse of the Congaree River emerges through the dense foliage. The trail now follows the river for over a mile, offering occasional glimpses of its flowing waters. While direct views from the trail are limited, you can enjoy breathtaking vistas from the sandbar, provided it's not flooded.

The riverbank is a remarkable feature, being one of the highest points in the floodplain. During floods, the river's sediment-laden waters overflow, depositing more sediment along the riverbank due to the sudden change in speed and direction. These larger, coarser-grained particles create distinct soil conditions, supporting a unique plant community. Trees like silver maple and ash-leaf maple dominate the overstory, while black walnut is a rare find in other parts of the park. The understory is dominated by spicebush, its branches arching over the trail. This shrub is known for its fragrant leaves and attractive red berries, which are a favorite of birds. It also serves as a host plant for the beautiful Spicebush Swallowtail butterfly.

The river's edge is a haven for birdlife, providing foraging and nesting opportunities. American Redstarts, typically found farther northwest, breed along the riverbank. Swainson's Warblers also thrive in the shrub cover, their secretive songs echoing through the forest.

Site 8: Sandbar

As you continue your journey, you'll come across a sign indicating a side trail leading to your left. This trail will take you to the sandbar. While it might seem like there's nothing there when the river level is moderate, don't be discouraged. Walk downstream for about 100 yards, and you'll likely find a substantial sandbar waiting for you. This is a great spot to take a break, relax, and explore.

The Sandbar: A Geological Wonder

The Congaree River has been shaping this landscape for thousands of years. As it meanders through the floodplain, it erodes ancient bluffs and deposits sediment, creating sandbars along the inner edges of its bends. These sandbars are constantly evolving, with coarse gravel at the upper end providing a suitable habitat for fish like the endangered Shortnose Sturgeon.

Flora and Fauna

Keep an eye out for the black willow trees and shrubs that are the first to colonize these sandbars. You might also find cockleburs, a favorite food of the extinct Carolina Parakeet. The sandbar is also home to a variety of freshwater mussels, including the threatened Yellow Lampmussel. Unfortunately, invasive species like the Asian clam have also found their way here.

As you explore, you may come across fragments of Native American pottery. These artifacts have been washed downstream from eroding riverbanks and offer a glimpse into the region's history. While it's tempting to collect them, it's important to remember that it's illegal to do so. Instead, take a photo to preserve the memory. These pottery sherds likely date back thousands of years, from the Archaic period to the Mississippian culture.

Birdwatching Opportunities

While you're on the sandbar, keep your eyes peeled for soaring birds of prey like Osprey, Anhinga, and Bald Eagles. You may also spot other species such as swallows, Belted Kingfishers, and Double-crested Cormorants flying overhead.

Site 9: Western Boundary Road and Boat Ramp

After leaving the sandbar, turn left to continue on the trail. Shortly after, the trail will turn right and join a gravel road (Western Boundary Road) that stretches north from the river to Old Bluff Road at the park's Bannister Bridge canoe/kayak landing. While most of Western Boundary Road lies on park property, private access is currently restricted to park visitors. However, there are plans to provide visitor access to this road from Bannister Bridge in the future.

Before continuing on the trail/road, take a detour south to inspect the boat ramp. Although sediment might make it challenging, this ramp offers a final glimpse of the river. Historically, the United States Hunt Club used this ramp for launching boats and transporting equipment across the river. As you continue your journey on the trail, you might notice old windlasses used to pull barges across the river. The club also maintained a small clubhouse here, in addition to its main clubhouse at the former hunt club clearing you passed earlier. It's worth noting that the USGS operates a river gauge at this location, which has been in use since the 1980s.

Turn around and head north on the River Trail/Western Boundary Road. This area of the park is known for its favorable habitat for Wild Turkeys, so keep your eyes peeled for these birds crossing the road.

Site 10: Trail Junction

As you navigate the River Trail, keep an eye out for a trail sign that indicates a right turn off the Western Boundary Road. This trail follows Hammond Gut and then Shallow Gut, leading you to the southern bank of Duck Pond. Along this stretch, you'll encounter substantial stands of switchcane. This plant plays a crucial role in the local ecosystem, providing nesting and foraging habitat for wildlife and acting as a host plant for various butterfly species.

Native Americans recognized the importance of canebrakes and used controlled fires to manage and promote their growth. These canebrakes were valuable for game, attracting various wildlife species. However, the arrival of early settlers led to a decline in canebrakes as they were used for livestock forage and cleared for agriculture. The presence of cane was often seen as an indicator of fertile soil, contributing to its removal.

Among the towering trees that line this portion of the trail, Swamp Chestnut Oak is a particularly common sight. Its light bark and large, sweet acorns make it easily recognizable. This tree, also known as Basket Oak or Cow Oak, has practical applications. Its wood is suitable for crafting baskets, while its acorns provide a valuable food source for animals.

Site 11: Duck Pond

The Duck Pond Trail offers a glimpse into the unique wetland ecosystem of Congaree National Park. As you venture along the boardwalk, you'll encounter the Duck Pond, a natural water body that was once part of the main Congaree River channel. Over time, this channel became cut off, forming a slough that is now dominated by water tupelo and baldcypress trees.

These two species are remarkably adapted to the wet conditions of the pond. Water tupelo trees have large leaves and distinctive curved trunks, while baldcypress trees boast straight trunks, feathery needles, and the prominent "knees" that emerge from the water. This lush wetland habitat provides an ideal home for Wood Ducks, and with a bit of luck, you might spot some swimming in the pond. Keep your ears open, too, as the hens' loud squawks will alert you to their presence even before you see them.

After exploring the Duck Pond, follow the trail back to the trail junction and retrace your steps to the Visitor Center. This short but scenic detour offers a memorable experience and a deeper appreciation for the diverse ecosystems found within Congaree National Park.

Difficulty: Moderate. The trail involves some elevation changes and can be challenging in hot weather.

Type of Hike: Loop

Dogs are welcomed but must be on leash

Kids are allowed but younger children may need assistance

Length: 10.4 miles

Estimated Time to Complete: 5-7 hours, depending on pace and stops.

Accessibility: The trail is generally accessible, but there are some uneven sections and boardwalks.

Trailhead Elevation: Approximately 50 feet

Total Elevation Gain: Approximately 45 feet

Highest Elevation: Approximately 95 feet

Ability: Suitable for hikers of moderate fitness levels.

Features: Old-growth hardwood forests, Congaree River, wildlife viewing opportunities, and potential for camping near the river.

Allowed Uses: Hiking

Trail Surface: Mostly dirt and gravel with some boardwalks.

Best Time to Hike: Spring and fall are generally considered the best times to hike due to pleasant temperatures and fewer crowds. However, the park is beautiful year-round.

Kingsnake Trail

Trailhead: Kingsnake Trail, Gadsden, SC 29052, USA.

Description:

The Kingsnake Trail, a secluded path within Congaree National Park, offers a unique and tranquil hiking experience. This trail, which is 3.6 miles long, connects to the park's main trail system and serves as a popular access point for canoeing and kayaking on Cedar Creek. While the trail itself is not a loop, the initial 1.2-mile portion provides a pleasant out-and-back walk through the floodplain.

The trail follows a logging road constructed in the 1970s. This logging activity reignited a conservation movement led by Harry Hampton to preserve the old-growth forest along the Congaree floodplain. Although the area has been selectively cut, many mature trees remain, including a remarkable cherrybark oak and a champion-class persimmon tree. The trail also crosses Cedar Creek, the only Outstanding National Resource Water in South Carolina.

As you hike, you may encounter various wildlife, such as wood ducks, barred owls, and the rare Rusty Blackbird. Additionally, you'll discover a large baldcypress and a cattle mound dating back to the 19th century. While the trail is named for the Eastern Kingsnake, sightings of this nocturnal reptile are uncommon.

To reach the Kingsnake Trail, follow National Park Road to Old Bluff Road, then turn right onto South Cedar Creek Road. Continue for 1.8 miles until you see the sign for South Cedar Creek Canoe Launch and Kingsnake Trail Access. The trail is generally easy to follow, although fallen trees and other obstacles may occasionally obscure the path. Keep an eye out for trail signs marked with the number "6" to stay on course.

The Kingsnake Trail offers a peaceful and rewarding hike through the heart of Congaree National Park. Discover hidden treasures, observe wildlife, and appreciate the beauty of this unique wilderness area.

106

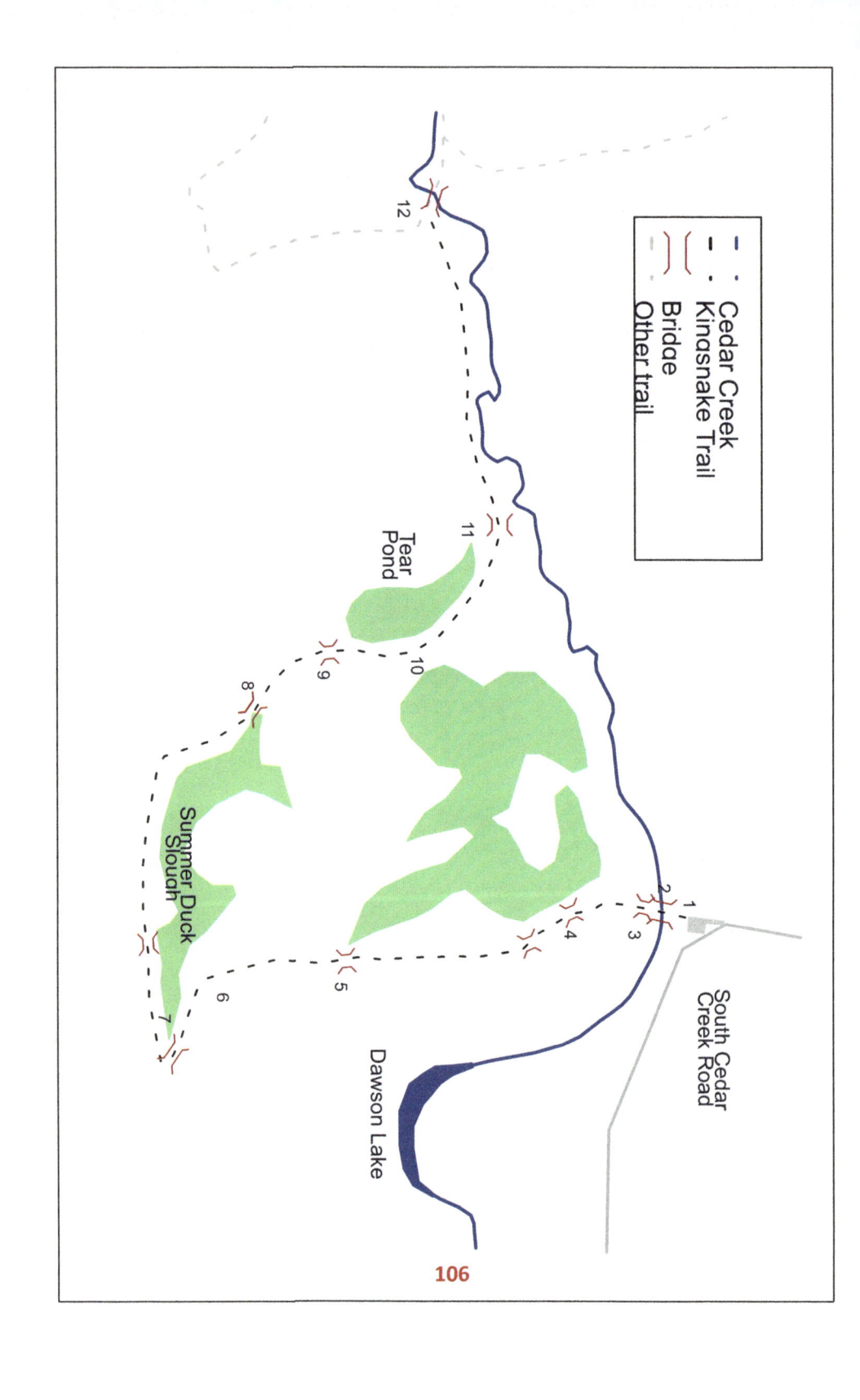

Site 1: Parking Lot

The parking lot is often an overlooked spot for birdwatchers. However, it can be a great place to observe a variety of feathered friends. In the summer, keep an eye out for Mississippi Kites soaring high above. These graceful birds are known for their acrobatic flying skills.

Butterfly Haven

Butterflies also frequent parking lots. The gravel surface provides a source of mineral salts that they need to supplement their diet. So, take a moment to scan the ground for these colorful insects.

Exploring the Trail

If the weather is pleasant, consider exploring the trail before heading to the kiosk. Cedar Creek and the Iron Bridge offer stunning natural beauty. And don't forget to take advantage of the pit toilet facilities if needed.

Site 2: Iron Bridge (Bridge L)

The trail begins along a logging road, known as the New Road, that was carved into the landscape in the 1970s. However, this path isn't entirely new. Historical records reveal that the initial segment of the New Road retraces the footsteps of a much older road, dating back to the late 18th century.

As you hike, take a moment to pause at the bridge overlooking Cedar Creek. This remarkable creek enters the park at Bannister Bridge and meanders gracefully across the floodplain for a distance of 15 miles before merging with the Congaree River. Cedar Creek holds a special significance, being the sole Outstanding National Resource Water within the state. Its exceptional natural beauty and recreational opportunities have earned it this prestigious recognition.

For those seeking a more aquatic adventure, canoes and kayaks can be launched on the Cedar Creek Wilderness Trail at two convenient locations within the park: Bannister Bridge and South Cedar Creek. The gentle current and ample width of the creek make it suitable for both downstream and upstream paddling, allowing visitors to explore the scenic waterways at their own pace. To learn more about the park's popular free paddling tours, feel free to contact the park directly.

Site 3: Second Bridge

This bridge traverses a small slough, a remnant of an old river or creek channel. Though no longer directly connected to a water source, sloughs typically retain water throughout the year, except during severe droughts. The park boasts a diverse array of trees adapted to thrive in these perpetually moist habitats within the floodplain. Among these, water tupelo and bald cypress stand out as the dominant canopy trees in these low-lying areas.

The majority of trees visible here are water tupelo, easily recognized by their substantial leaves and sinuous trunks. Bald cypress, another iconic tree of Southern wetlands, is also present. It is distinguished by its notably straight trunk, feathery needles, and the numerous "knees" that protrude from the ground around its base.

Site 4: Third Bridge

As you cross the Whiskey Pond Gut Bridge, take a moment to appreciate the unique landscape of Congaree National Park. This bridge spans a small, seasonal stream known locally as a "gut." Guts are shallow, short floodplain streams that often dry up during the summer months. They play a crucial role in the park's flood cycle, transporting water from the Congaree River throughout the floodplain and then helping to channel it back into the river as the floodwaters recede.

The Ancient Bald Cypress

On your right, you'll notice a towering bald cypress tree. This species is renowned for its slow decay, earning it the nickname "the wood eternal." Historically, bald cypress was highly valued for its timber, used in everything from buildings to shingles. Unfortunately, excessive logging in the 19th and 20th centuries decimated many of the old-growth bald cypress forests in the southeastern United States. The trees you see in Congaree National Park are among the last remaining examples of this majestic species.

Site 5: Fifth Bridge

As you embark on the trail from the third bridge to the fifth bridge, you'll be traversing a section of the forest that was selectively logged in the 1970s. Despite the past logging activity, the area has shown remarkable resilience. Towering canopy trees, including sweetgum, hickory, and oak, still dominate the landscape, creating a sense of awe and wonder.

The late summer months bring a vibrant transformation to this section of the trail. Longleaf Lobelia flowers carpet the ground, their bright blooms attracting a diverse array of butterflies. Keep your eyes peeled for the delicate Lace-winged Roadside Skipper and the striking Zabulon Skipper, often observed nectaring on the same bloom stalk.

Site 6: (Optional) Moccasin Pond Baldcypress

For those seeking a unique experience, a short off-trail excursion to the Lone Cypress of Whiskey Pond offers a rewarding detour. However, this adventure should only be undertaken with a working compass or GPS, as it's easy to become disoriented in the park's terrain.

Finding the Cypress

To locate the cypress, keep an eye out for an exposed galvanized culvert pipe on the trail. An arm of Whiskey Pond will be visible to your right. Once you've identified this spot, look behind you and you'll see a trail marker with coordinates N 33.8176, W -80.6465.

Navigating the Woods

Enter the woods to your left and follow a small channel in a westerly direction. Another channel will appear on your right. Stay between these channels, and you'll soon reach Moccasin Pond. Keep the bank edge 50 to 75 yards to your left, and you'll encounter the Lone Cypress within a couple hundred yards.

The Cypress and Its Knees

The cypress is a remarkable sight, with a prominent "foot" and a palisade of cypress knees surrounding it. The purpose of these knees is still a subject of scientific debate. Some believe they enhance the stability of the root system, while recent research suggests they may play a role in gas exchange during periods of flooding.

Returning to the Trail

Once you've admired the cypress, retrace your steps west to the trail and continue your journey.

Site 7: Bridge K and Summer Duck Slough

Bridge K is a significant landmark on the trail. It spans a small gut that connects Summer Duck Slough to Big Snake Slough. After crossing the bridge, the trail takes a sharp turn to the right, heading westward. The old logging road, however, continues straight ahead. While the logging road may be tempting to explore, it's important to note that it's unmaintained and overgrown with switchcane. It's advisable to avoid this route unless you're accompanied by someone familiar with the area.

Following the South Bank of Summer Duck Slough

For the next mile, you'll be walking along the south bank of Summer Duck Slough. This slough is named after the Wood Duck, also known as the "Summer Duck" due to its breeding habits in the southeast. The male Wood Duck is renowned for its striking beauty and can often be found in the park's waterbodies. Keep your eyes peeled, as you might encounter these elegant birds, often in pairs. Remember, Wood Ducks are quite alert and will likely spot you before you see them. You might hear the hen's alarm call and only catch a glimpse of the birds flying away.

Navigating the Fallen Trees

When I visited, this portion of the trail had several fallen trees that required careful maneuvering. Be sure to keep an eye out for trail markers to ensure you stay on the correct path. It's important to remember that Summer Duck Slough and its well-defined bank edge are always on your right. If you encounter obstacles, it's generally safer to find detours to the right rather than venturing to the left.

Site 8: Eight Bridge

As you continue your journey along the trail, you'll start noticing a familiar sight: pine trees. This marks the end of your walk along Summer Duck Slough. The eighth bridge, a small structure crossing a gut connecting Big Slough and the northwestern end of Summer Duck Slough, is a notable landmark.

Nearby, you'll find Cooner's Mound, one of seven cattle mounds in the park listed on the National Register of Historic Places. This well-shaped rectangular mound was constructed by slaves in the 19th century as a refuge for free-range livestock during floods. The Congaree River's flooding can inundate the entire floodplain, especially in winter and early spring. Although floods usually subside after a few days, livestock herded to mounds would still require hay delivered by boat.

Beyond the eighth bridge, pay close attention to the trail markers. There are a few shallow channels that intersect the path, and it's easy to accidentally veer off the trail and follow these channels instead.

Site 9: Bridge J

As you continue your trek, the trail leads you across Bridge J, where it gracefully spans Circle Gut. After crossing the bridge, the trail takes a sharp right turn, offering a new perspective on the surrounding landscape.

Soon, you'll be greeted by the picturesque sight of Tear Pond, a large, tear-shaped slough that stretches out to your left. The trail follows the pond's bank, providing a serene and intimate view of its tranquil waters.

The dominant vegetation around Tear Pond is Water Tupelo, whose tall, slender trunks and feathery leaves create a lush and verdant canopy. However, you'll also notice a few Baldcypress trees scattered throughout the area, particularly along the pond's edge near the trail. These majestic trees, with their distinctive buttressed trunks and feathery foliage, add a touch of diversity to the landscape.

Site 10: Cherrybark Oak

As you journey along Tear Pond, a breathtaking sight awaits: an immense Cherrybark Oak tree. This majestic giant is one of the largest hardwoods in the park, boasting a staggering diameter of over 22 feet. While its crown has suffered some damage over the years, it still stands as a testament to the enduring power of nature.

The Cherrybark Oak is a particularly valuable hardwood, prized for its use in veneer production for the furniture industry. Its wood is renowned for its beauty and durability, making it a sought-after commodity. As you admire this ancient tree, take a moment to appreciate the incredible diversity and natural beauty that surrounds you in the park.

Site 11: Cedar Creek

Begin your journey by following the trail along Tear Pond. As you continue, you'll eventually find yourself back at Cedar Creek. From here, the trail turns left and follows the creek for approximately a half-mile. This portion of the trail offers a chance to admire some truly remarkable trees.

Champion Trees: A Hidden Gem

While champion trees come in various sizes, there's a particularly impressive Persimmon tree near the trail. This tree is easily recognizable by its distinctive checkered black bark. If you look carefully to your left as the trail veers away from the creek's edge, especially during the winter when foliage isn't obstructing the view, you might spot this 8-foot circumference Persimmon. Once a national co-champion, this tree stands tall at 110 feet, a testament to its remarkable size and health.

Navigating the Downed Trees

As you continue along the trail, you'll encounter an area with several large downed trees. Be sure to stay alert for trail markers and take any necessary detours to the right along Cedar Creek. Once you've navigated this section, look to your left for a massive Water Oak with a circumference of nearly 18 feet. Despite its name, Water Oak is a versatile species that thrives in various soil conditions. While other oak species are more common in the park, Water Oak, along with Laurel Oak, Swamp Chestnut Oak, Willow Oak, and Cherrybark Oak, dominate the canopy of many of the park's diverse vegetation communities.

Site 12: Junction with the Oakridge Trail

If you've reached the junction with the Oakridge Trail, you have the option of returning the way you came. This will involve walking 3.6 miles back to your starting point.

Continuing to the Visitor Center

For those who have arranged a car shuttle, continuing to the Visitor Center is a viable option. This route adds another 1.9 miles to your journey.

Following the Oakridge Trail

To reach the Visitor Center, follow the Oakridge Trail over Bridge I. Once you've crossed the bridge, you'll connect with the Weston Lake Loop Trail.

Taking the Weston Lake Loop Trail

Turn right onto the Weston Lake Loop Trail and continue following it until you reach the Boardwalk Loop. You can choose to walk the Boardwalk Loop in either direction, as both paths will eventually lead you to the Visitor Center.

Difficulty: Easy

Type of hike: Out and back

Dogs are allowed but must be kept on leash.

Kids are allowed

Length in miles: 7.8

Estimated time to complete: 2-3 hours

Accessibility: The trail is accessible to wheelchairs and strollers

Trailhead Elevation: 48 feet

Total Elevation Gain: 22 feet

Highest Elevation: 50 feet

Ability: Beginner

Feature: Scenic

Allowed uses: Hiking

Trail surface: Dirt

Best time to hike: Spring and fall

Glossary

Slough is a wetland or swamp, often characterized by:

- **Shallow water:** The water in a slough is typically shallow, often with muddy or marshy bottoms.
- **Slow-moving water:** The water flow is usually slow, sometimes stagnant.
- **Reeds and grasses:** Sloughs are often covered in reeds, grasses, or other aquatic plants.

Switchcane (Arundinaria tecta) is a perennial, woody grass native to the southeastern United States. It's a member of the bamboo family and is known for its tall, hollow stems and dense, thicket-like growth.

Trail difficulty - refers to a rating system that helps hikers choose trails that are appropriate for their fitness level and experience. Here's a breakdown of common trail difficulty categories:

- **Easy:** Easy trails are generally short (less than 2 miles) and have a flat or gentle incline. They are suitable for hikers of all ages and fitness levels, including young children and families.
- **Moderate:** Moderate trails are moderately challenging and may be longer (2 to 4 miles) with some steeper sections and elevation gain. They are suitable for hikers in good physical condition who are comfortable walking for a few hours.
- **Challenging:** Challenging trails are more difficult and may be longer (4+ miles) with significant elevation gain, steep inclines, and uneven terrain. They require good physical fitness and some experience hiking on challenging terrain.

- **Strenuous:** Strenuous trails are the most difficult and are typically long (4+ miles) with significant elevation gain, steep inclines, and difficult terrain. They require excellent physical fitness, strong hiking skills, and experience navigating difficult trails.

Elevation change - This is the overall variation in height you'll experience on the trail. It considers both going up (elevation gain) and going down (elevation loss).

Features- is simply any interesting or noteworthy aspect of the trail itself. This could include things like scenic overlooks, waterfalls, wildflowers, or historical markers.

Loop Hike - is a more intricate and diverse form of hiking. As the name suggests, in a Loop hike, you start and finish at the same trailhead, but you follow a circuitous route that doesn't require retracing your steps. Here are the characteristics that make Loop hikes appealing:

1. **Variety**: Loop hikes offer a rich diversity of scenery, as you traverse different terrains, ecosystems, and vistas. You won't see the same section of the trail twice.

2. **Sense of Accomplishment**: Completing a loop hike often feels more satisfying, as you've circumnavigated a specific area and returned to your starting point without repeating any segments of the trail.

3. **Adventure**: The element of uncertainty and exploration is more prominent in loop hikes, as you might not know exactly what's around each bend. This adds excitement and a spirit of adventure to the experience.

4. **Efficiency**: Loop hikes make efficient use of your time and energy since they don't require doubling back. This

can be especially appealing when you have a limited amount of time for your hike.

However, Loop hikes also have their challenges, such as potentially more complex navigation and the need for good trail markers. Some hikers might find the unpredictability of the terrain and the possibility of getting lost a bit daunting.

Out and Back Hike

The "Out and Back" hike, also known as a "there and back" hike, is one of the simplest and most straightforward hiking formats. In this type of hike, you begin at a designated trailhead and travel along the path until you decide to turn around and return to your starting point. Here are some key features of Out and Back hikes:

1. **Simplicity**: Out and Back hikes are ideal for beginners and those who prefer a straightforward, no-fuss approach. Since you retrace your steps, navigation is often more straightforward, reducing the chances of getting lost.

2. **Predictable Terrain**: Knowing that you'll return on the same trail means you have a good understanding of the terrain. This allows you to plan and pace your hike more accurately.

3. **Scenic Views**: Out and Back hikes often lead you to the same stunning viewpoints on your return journey, offering a different perspective of the landscape you've just traversed.

4. **Flexibility**: You can customize the length of your hike by choosing how far you want to venture from the trailhead, making it suitable for hikers of all levels.

However, there are limitations to Out and Back hikes. The monotony of retracing your steps can become less engaging for some, and the predictability of the terrain might not provide the variety that loop hikes offer.

Point to Point Hike

Refers to a hike that starts at one location and ends at a different location. This means you won't be following the same path back to your starting point like you would with a loop trail. Because of this, point-to-point hikes often require some logistical planning to get back to your car or starting point.

Key features:

1. **Transportation:** You'll need a way to get back to where you parked your car at the beginning of the hike. This could involve arranging a shuttle service with a friend, using public transportation if available, or having another car pick you up at the end point.

2. **Multi-day hikes:** Point-to-point trails are commonly used for multi-day backpacking trips, where you camp overnight along the way.

Overlook - refers to a specific location on a trail that offers a particularly scenic or panoramic view of the surrounding landscape. These are often high points, such as cliffs or mountain summits, that provide unobstructed vistas.

Hikers often aim for overlooks as a reward for their effort on the trail. They can be a great place to take a break, enjoy the scenery, and snap some pictures.

Trailhead – refers to the starting point of a trail. It's essentially the place where you leave the road or developed area and begin your trek on the designated path.

Made in the USA
Coppell, TX
24 March 2025